Exceptional

BUILD YOUR PERSONAL HIGHLIGHT REEL
AND UNLOCK YOUR POTENTIAL

DANIEL M. CABLE

CHRONICLE PRISM

Library of Congress Cataloging-in-Publication Data
Names: Cable, Daniel M. (Daniel Merle)
Title: Exceptional : build your personal highlight reel and unlock your
    potential / by Daniel M. Cable.
Description: 1st Edition. | San Francisco : Chronicle Prism, 2020. |
    Includes bibliographical references. |
Identifiers: LCCN 2020015212 | ISBN 9781452184258 (hardback) | ISBN
    9781797201559 (ebook)
Subjects: LCSH: Self-actualization (Psychology) | Self-confidence. |
    Resilience (Personality trait)
Classification: LCC BF637.S4 C3125 2020 | DDC 158—dc23
LC record available at https://lccn.loc.gov/2020015212

Manufactured in the United States of America.

Interior Design by Pamela Geismar.
Typesetting by Happenstance Type-O-Rama.
Cover design by Kathleen Lynch / Black Kat Design.

Names in this book have been changed to ensure privacy and confidentiality.

10 9 8 7 6 5 4 3 2 1

Chronicle books and gifts are available at special quantity discounts to corporations, professional associations, literacy programs, and other organizations. For details and discount information, please contact our premiums department at corporatesales@chroniclebooks.com or at 1-800-759-0190.

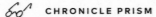 CHRONICLE PRISM

Chronicle Prism is an imprint of Chronicle Books LLC, 680 Second Street, San Francisco, California 94107

www.chronicleprism.com

TO ALISON, DAISY, AND VIOLET

CONTENTS

Introduction

At age nineteen, Rebecca could not find her way around the block. As described by neurologist Oliver Sacks, when getting dressed to go outside, Rebecca might spend an hour jamming a hand into the wrong glove and wasn't able to unlock the front door on her own. Her grandmother, who had raised her from age three, said she was "just like a child" in many ways. Rebecca had always felt that others focused on her many limitations, often making fun of her, and as a result she was painfully shy and withdrawn.

When Sacks first met Rebecca he saw her as a casualty, a broken creature. As part of a clinical program, she had done appallingly in her testing. Like his colleagues before him, Sacks could easily pick out and dissect her neurological impairments, breakdowns, and intellectual limitations.

The next time Sacks saw Rebecca, however, it was very different. Instead of a test situation, he had come across her on a park bench on a warm spring day. Rebecca sat, gazing at the April foliage with obvious delight. Sacks wrote, "Her posture had none of the clumsiness which had so impressed me before. Sitting there, in a light dress, her face calm and slightly smiling . . . she could have been any young woman enjoying a beautiful spring day." As Sacks approached, she turned and gave him a broad smile. The words she spoke came out in poetic spurts, odd and sudden: "spring," "birth," "seasons," and "everything in its time."

The goal of the clinical tests had been to measure and reveal Rebecca's insufficiencies. However, the tests gave no insight into her positive abilities. As Sacks began to understand Rebecca better, he also saw her core strengths. There were times when, compared to her own average, Rebecca was *exceptional*.

When she danced, for example, all her clumsiness disappeared. While emotionally disengaged during her testing, outside the clinic she was affectionate and showed deep attachment to her grandmother. She had a love for nature, spending many happy hours in city parks and botanical gardens. Although she was unable to read or write, Rebecca responded to poetry when it was read to her. And at times, like that spring day, she used beautiful, apt metaphors.

Superficially, Rebecca was a mass of incapacities, but at a deeper level there was a sense of calm and completeness, of being fully aware and alive.

The clinical program pressured Rebecca into a variety of improvement workshops and classes that simply didn't work for her. While the goal was to help her, and patients like her, become more efficient and functional in everyday tasks, Sacks observed, "What we did was to drive them full-tilt upon their limitations, as had already been done, futilely, and often to the point of cruelty, throughout their lives." For many decades the fields of psychology and neurology have far too often focused on people's defects and how to fix them. Rebecca had spent the last nineteen years living with her limitations, and these tests and classes served as a constant reminder of where she didn't meet society's conventional standards.

After her grandmother died, Rebecca said she would have no more classes. As she put it, "The classes, the odd jobs, have no meaning." When Sacks asked what might work better, she said she loved the theater. Sacks removed Rebecca from the classes and instead enrolled her in a special theater group. Rebecca began to thrive. Sacks wrote, "It composed her; she did amazingly well: she became a complete person . . . the theatre group soon became her life."

We all are limited in so many ways. Like Rebecca, none of us is perfect physically, psychologically, or emotionally. And often we focus on our many limitations. In fact, it is our first instinct to start with critical self-evaluation.

We work hard to identify and emphasize our weaknesses because, through practice and effort, we can improve some of our personal shortcomings and move them toward the "average" of other people. And because of this, many of us drive ourselves full-tilt upon our own limitations, often to the point of self-cruelty.

Marcus Buckingham, author of *Now, Discover Your Strengths*, called this approach "remediation." Remediation is working hard to improve from being "terrible" at something to being "not too bad." Sure, we all need to keep improving the areas in our lives that hold us back. But when we spend all our resources and time *fixing ourselves*, our achievements become only a frustrated mush of mediocrity across things for which we had little interest in the first place. Anything done in excellence is because people are playing to their strengths, not working on remediation. It is hard to thrive when we are investing the majority of our energy in preventing failure, when we are playing not to lose.

Like Rebecca, to find our best "functionality" in this world—to make our best impact—we need to start with what we do right, and find a way to do more of that. If we had endless time, maybe we eventually could conquer all our weaknesses. But guess what? Our lives are not infinite. The question is, "Given my limited time, what is the best impact I am capable of making in this life?"

This book will focus on what we can accomplish when we use our signature strengths and discover the powerful qualities that are unique to us. You will construct a life that feels whole, meaningful, and alive, as you discover how to increase your contributions to the world around you and the relationships that matter most. Each of us can bring forth a version of ourselves that is uniquely outstanding. It's a version of ourselves that already exists—all we have to do is access it more often.

A PERSONAL HIGHLIGHT REEL

Imagine waking up, switching on the television, and seeing your best moments from the day before being aired. You'd watch the part of that meeting where you made an incredible point that inspired people to really listen. And that brief chat with your daughter that sent her off to school feeling ready to give her first big presentation. And when you decided to reinterpret your partner's comment as helpful instead of critical, which led to a conversation instead of a fight.

As you watched these moments, you'd relive the experiences where you were closest to your full potential and the positive emotions they evoked. You'd also learn how to repeat those moments of excellence. This is your own *personal highlight reel*.

You are likely more familiar with highlight reels when it comes to sports clips, replaying the biggest and best performances of a specific athlete. Unfortunately, most of us are never going to see our peak moves aired on ESPN, but over the next eleven chapters you will learn how to build a highlight reel for yourself. Composed of your most exceptional moments throughout your life, both large and small, your highlight reel will contain your own memories, combined with memories from people who know you well. Integrating materials and evidence from many different sources, this reel will help you recognize your strengths, shape your life around them, and create new habits that trigger the best version of who you are, more of the time.

Through a consultancy I cofounded called Essentic, I've helped tens of thousands of people create highlight reels to learn about themselves at their best. In my career as a professor of organizational behavior, I've been conducting research for nearly a decade that showcases just how personal highlight reels can transform our lives.

Consider a study I did with Fran Gino at Harvard University and Brad Staats at the University of North Carolina. We recruited participants to work on a series of tasks in a lab at Harvard and introduced them to the lab's culture and goals in an orientation. Before they got started on their tasks, we told one group of people to write what they learned about the lab so far. We instructed a second group to write about their *Personal Highlight Reel,* asking them to "reflect on a specific time—perhaps on a job, perhaps at home— when you were acting the way you were 'born to act.'"

Compared to the people who wrote about the lab, the group who wrote about personal highlights felt more "unique" and "authentic." And these feelings affected their behaviors. They demonstrated better stamina, working longer on the tasks with far fewer mistakes than the other group.

When we replicated this study at Wipro—a technology company in India—new employees who wrote about their personal highlights were 32% less likely to quit within six months and also were actively finding ways to make their customers happier. Together, these studies show how focusing on our highlights makes us feel more authentic, which increases our feelings of resilience and satisfaction.

Highlight reels not only help you be more productive, but they also show you how to pursue your dreams with more confidence as you become more self-aware of where you excel. This is why world-class athletes use them, and just like an athlete, you will curate memories of your own peak performances that you can replay mentally whenever you need them.

When we watch *SportsCenter*, we all know of course that the athlete is not *always* as good as his or her highlight reel. We all have good days and bad days. We all have weaknesses and limitations. But rather than focus on what we do wrong, a highlight reel captures what we do right.

Personal highlight reels are powerful because they connect the images of exceptional performance held in your mind with your actual behaviors, transforming your stories into reality. Jack

Nicklaus, sometimes called the Golden Bear and often called the greatest golfer of all time, wrote in his book *Golf My Way*:

> *I never hit a shot, even in practice, without having a very sharp, in-focus picture of it in my head. It's like a color movie. First I "see" the ball where I want it to finish, nice and white and sitting up high on the bright green grass. Then I "see" the ball going there; its path, trajectory, even its behavior on landing. The next scene shows me making the kind of swing that will turn the previous images into reality.*

Jack Nicklaus used imagery to focus his concentration and see himself at his best. This type of imagery is used by 86% of US Olympic sport psychologists in their athlete training programs. Successful Olympic athletes report that imagery is a consistent part of their mental preparation and training, where the goal is to recreate a successful experience in their minds, oftentimes crafting a mental play-by-play that involves all their senses. For example, a soccer player might use a mental highlight reel to "see" the opponents coming toward her as she goes to kick the ball, to "feel" the muscles in her legs as she gets ready to kick, and to "hear" the sound of the ball as she kicks it perfectly.

This is more than just wishful thinking, because this athlete is tapping into her actual behaviors that are true to her strengths. This is exactly what you will discover how to do for yourself when you create your personal highlight reel. These memories remind us what we are capable of at our best, building our confidence and giving us a road map to return to that success over and over again.

HOW TO USE THIS BOOK

Throughout this book you will learn about a new approach I have spent almost a decade developing called the *positive method*, which is based on my research and uses science to help you craft a well-lived life. This three-step method helps people tap into their potential. It is a tried and proven method that I teach in my classes at London Business School, and that I continue to use in my own life.

This three-step process identifies your strengths and helps you chronically access your powerful qualities—and ultimately reveals how living up to your full potential can improve the relationships you value the most, as well as the world around you.

Step 1 breaks down the science behind best-self activation. You will learn to recognize what story you're currently telling yourself about who you are and discover how to edit that story to reflect your best possible self. This step will give you the confidence to create your highlight reel. Some parts of this journey can feel awkward and unusual, which pushes us away from our potential. It's important to have the confidence to push back.

Step 2 has three activities that result in your highlight reel:

- *Reflect* and "mine your mind" for stories about yourself that you are most proud of and that you find remarkable. After all, we know how it feels, inside, when we are using our strengths and making our most meaningful impact.

- *Give gratitude* to people in your social network for times they have been at their best. This science-backed approach strengthens your relationships and creates fulfilling connections with others.

- *Gather evidence* from your social network in the form of their stories and memories of your brightest and most outstanding moments. You'll gain grounded evidence about your core strengths.

Step 3 is learning how to access those signature strengths regularly. You'll learn how to create new lifelong habits that utilize your greatest qualities and craft a life around what you do best.

When you discover what environments lift you up, which relationships fuel your finest traits, and which of your strengths create positive change in the world, you'll find more energy, fulfillment, and confidence in everything you do. This is what tens of thousands of people have already experienced through the positive method. Just as they have, you will create a life you are proud to live.

It's what we all want, but it's so easy to lose our mojo as we get stuck in the doldrums of routine. You've been there, and I've been there. This is why we need tools to help us break out.

WAKING UP TO LIFE

When I was thirty-six years old, I was swimming in the natatorium at the University of North Carolina. With each stroke I felt something was off. Something was "catching" with my left arm. When I looked in the mirror after the swim, I found this lump on my neck by my clavicle. It was visible, big enough that it was restricting my stroke. Big enough that I wondered how I had not noticed it before. I thought, *just a swollen lymph node*. Like you get when you're fighting illness. Which I guess in a way it was.

But that night we had friends over to dinner, one of whom was a nurse. I mentioned it to her and she told me, "Dan, those ones aren't supposed to swell." The gravity in her voice made me go that week to get it checked out.

A few weeks later, when the doctor at the hospital sat me down for the results, she put her hand on my arm. I thought, *Hm. Seems serious*. When she said "lymphoma," the words hit me in a way that somehow seemed physical. "Cancer," describing me, was shocking. I definitely was not ready to hear "Stage 4." The floor opened up under me and in my panic I couldn't catch myself from falling. I tumbled down into a hole. I can still remember that feeling of falling.

During the next six months, I felt panic about dying. It was like my brain was trying to escape the facts. I mean, we all *know* we're going to die someday. But suddenly, death was more than a philosophical concept.

My daughters were one and three years old. What hurt me the most was the idea of not being able to watch them grow up. I was absolutely *furious* about that.

Fast-forward another six months: The chemo paid off. The tumor melted away. Basically, I got lucky because I was born after we humans had invented chemotherapy. It's a trick of fate: If I'd been born twenty years earlier, I wouldn't have seen my kids grow up.

This journey was scary for me, but the trauma had this incredible way of stripping away all the bullshit of my life. It is easier to see what matters to you when you know you don't have much time left.

I realized my life looked great on paper. I had a prestigious job as a business professor and consultant, making loads of money with a nice house and a wonderful family. But there were lots of cracks that I was working hard to not see. I was making a good living, but I wasn't feeling good about the life I had made. I had become bored, and I felt like I had been "waiting to live," as if I had assumed I would have unlimited time.

My experience of drawing up close to death helped me see—or I should say helped me *admit*—that I had been sleepwalking my way through life. I had been going through the motions. I had not been focused on using my core strengths.

I did not try to stall out. From the outside it looked like I was succeeding at life. But inside, it was like I had pressed cruise control. The result was that my potential was being wasted. The logical part of my brain rationalized this away because I was efficiently meeting conventional goals.

Promotions? *Check.*

Family? *Check.*

Second house? *Check.*

But whose benchmarks were these? With my new lens on life, I saw that I had overlooked the urgency to make my best impact, to act on my potential. For years, I had known that I had been giving less than I could. I didn't wake up to my own life until two events happened.

First, I recognized the transience of life. Second, I learned the scientific research behind using our strengths to live more fully. Together these events helped me make some serious changes that allowed me to develop the positive method and to pursue the life I had always wanted.

Just like Rebecca, we have to create our own standards of what a well-lived life feels and looks like. It is personal, individualized, and uniquely yours to decide. When you understand what strengths elate you, and then live by your measure of greatness, you become your own version of exceptional.

STEP 1

CHAPTER 1

Start with What We Do Right

Many of us think the best path to self-improvement is to face the cold truth about ourselves at our worst. We believe criticism is the most effective way to motivate change. This is why many people's initial instinct is to fight against the positive method, because it is a process that asks us to focus purely on what we do well.

As a professor of organizational behavior, I work with students and executives who come to the London Business School to maximize their leadership impact. And when they arrive, they usually expect to learn what they are doing wrong. They assume I will reveal which dimensions of leadership they score the worst on, and this will motivate them to grit their teeth and grind away at those weaknesses.

Actually, neuroscience tells us the opposite happens when people receive lots of negative feedback. Sharp criticism of the self will prompt threat and anxiety, often triggering the amygdala in the brain to release the stress hormone cortisol. A common result is that people "lock up" as the body prepares for defense. Or even worse, they feel overwhelmed and helpless. These negative emotions repel personal change.

When people feel defensive and threatened, they revert back to old habits rather than experiment with new behaviors. People learn and evolve when they have a safe place for self-exploration. This is how change happens: When we refocus our attention on our strengths, and lean into the positive momentum it creates, we are motivated to push ourselves harder, to try new things and take steps that lead to personal transformation.

This is where your personal highlight reel comes in, because it reflects stories and evidence of your strengths—of you at your best.

Peter Dowrick, a professor of psychiatry at the University of Auckland, observed the effect of personal highlight reels in a workshop for young adults with difficulties finding employment due to physical disabilities. In the workshop, people were given a series of individual assembly tasks to complete over the span of two weeks. One group of individuals watched themselves each workday on videotapes that showed them doing these assembly tasks—except that their mistakes and excess hesitations were edited out. Another group of individuals received financial incentives for each 10% increase in output in the assembly tasks. Over two weeks, productivity rose 15% for individuals who watched their highlight reel, but only 3% for those who got incentives. These trends were still in place four months later.

It is motivating to model our behaviors around peak performances. When we use methods like a personal highlight reel to reinforce our strengths, we build real and lasting confidence in our abilities that can help us perform even better in the future. We also feel deeper satisfaction with our identities and empowered to step into our potential.

Focusing on our core values and strengths also activates a part of our brain that releases powerful motivational chemicals like dopamine. In order to reprogram our minds to prioritize strengths over weaknesses, it helps to understand the power that giving positive feedback has on others and how impactful it can be to receive it.

GRATITUDE VISITS

Humans are so strange with the timing of our gratitude and appreciation for one another. So often we wait until the end of someone's life to praise them for the impact they've had on us. This means most of us never hear, or understand, the positive and profound influence we have on other people. Why do we wait until it's too late?

Dela, a funeral insurance company in the Netherlands, recognized that "the most beautiful words are often spoken to someone after that someone passes away." So, Dela gave people a chance to publicly express gratitude to someone living that they really cared about. Dela filmed the exchanges and aired these moments as TV commercials. In one of these gratitude videos, a twenty-year-old woman stood up at a sports event that her parents were attending and publicly thanked them for moving their family from Iran to the Netherlands in order to provide her with the freedom to pursue an education. As her parents sat there looking stunned and breathless, their daughter acknowledged them for making her dreams come true: "I want to thank you for your courage and perseverance, and for everything you have done for me."

If you get a chance to watch these exchanges online, you'll find they are both emotional and awkward. It is really interesting to observe the people who are hearing their family and friends express gratitude about them. Their faces contort, as they try to evade the bittersweet emotions that they feel. Their fingers try to push away the unexpected tears that come to their eyes. How uncomfortable they seem during such a *lovely* event.

It's a very powerful thing, when people remind us of how we touched their lives and of who we are in our best moments. Yet both sides of this event—the giver and the recipient—feel exposed and vulnerable as they share their appreciation for one another.

But in these Dela videos it is clear that the giver *wants* to thank them. They are expressing something they have wanted to tell them for years, maybe even decades. And you can tell that the recipients definitely *want* to hear what is being said. They are hanging on to every word, and it is affecting them profoundly. Without the Dela scheme, however, these beautiful exchanges would not have happened.

Dela's idea is similar to the gratitude visit invented by Martin Seligman, a professor, author, and someone who has often been referred to as "the father of positive psychology." I first read about Seligman's gratitude visits at a very special time in my life. I had just begun to wean myself off chemotherapy and was starting to allow myself to believe I might still have some life left in me. This research had a huge impact on my own research identity and the creation of the positive method.

In these gratitude visits, Seligman's participants wrote a detailed letter to someone who had made a significant impact on their lives. They told a story that explained in concrete terms what the person did, and why they were grateful. They described what made that person's actions so valuable and unique to them.

Seligman then had the participants visit those people and read their letters aloud to them. He suggested that they take their time reading the letter, so both parties could savor it. Seligman said the exercise was always very moving for both people involved: "Everyone cries when you do a gratitude visit."

The empirical research showed that these gratitude visits increased quality of life for both the writer and the recipient. A full month after the visit, they were still experiencing substantially more joy in their lives. They also experienced substantially less depressive symptoms, compared to a control group who were told to live their lives as usual, without any intervention.

Even more importantly, both the giver and the receiver of the gratitude visit felt closer to each other after the experience. And people who were thanked often started thanking others. The result is a self-motivating chain of gratitude and positive memories being shared among more and more people.

But for the most part, people aren't in the habit of highlighting others' unique contributions, or sharing positive feedback freely.

Later in the book, we'll talk about the science behind why such a beautiful thing can feel so uncomfortable or socially awkward and how we can move past it.

Around the same period of time that I discovered Seligman's gratitude visits, I read about another positive psychology approach recommended by Laura Morgan Roberts and her colleagues at the University of Michigan. Roberts's approach struck me as similar in some ways to Seligman's, because they both help people learn about their best impact on others. However, Roberts suggested that we should be proactive rather than wait for people to give us a gratitude visit (which, let's be honest, might not happen for a long time). She recommended that if we want to understand our unique impact on others, we should reach out to our friends, family, and colleagues and ask them to write down their memories about us at our best.

Roberts and her team called this approach a Reflected Best-Self Exercise. These memories written by the important people in your life act as a mirror, reflecting your positive impact back to you. You might get twenty or twenty-five stories from ten different people. Together, these stories are something like your eulogy, except you get to hear them while you're still alive!

What I love about Roberts's approach is that it allows you to see yourself through other people's eyes. And, these are people that you trust and respect. Their stories help you remember, and re-experience, moments when you were at your very best. Because, like Rebecca in the introduction, we all have limitations, but we also all have moments where we shine. We all have times when we make a bigger, better impact on the people in our lives and the world. We all have moments when we are exceptional.

Some people call it "being in flow" or "in your zone." You could say you are approaching your own potential during those moments.

Of course, it's not all the time. For lots of us, it's not even every day. Most days, we're at our personal average. There is nothing wrong with that. Your personal average may be first-rate, much better than my daily average. But sometimes, you are exceptional, even by your standards.

Roberts's exercise focuses on a large number of contributors from different parts of our social network. Seligman's exercise is a one-to-one personal meeting. But in both exercises, people who we care about tell us their fondest memories of us. They give us narratives of when we are extraordinary. They help build our personal highlight reel.

Both exercises are powered by gratitude and the gift of hearing our own eulogy.

As you read about Roberts's and Seligman's exercises, you might find yourself resisting the idea of focusing only on the positive. Many people ask, "Shouldn't we at least balance the best-self stories with some stories about people at their worst?" In other words, don't we need to show people their limitations along with their strengths? The answer is no. Because that is not how our brains work. If you show people both strengths and weaknesses, they will focus on the weaknesses.

Why is this?

Our brains have evolved to concentrate on negative information first. Research shows that negative events (losing money, being abandoned by friends, or receiving criticism) grab our attention more than positive events of the same type (winning money, gaining friends, or receiving praise). We tune in to bad emotions and bad feedback much more than good. We process negative information more thoroughly than positive information.

Of course, addressing our limitations and flaws sometimes is necessary. But remediation is a very different exercise from thriving. Prevention of failure rarely leads to excellence. This is why, if we want to learn how to become our best more often, we are not going to highlight limitations and flaws in our highlight reels.

Both Seligman's gratitude visits and Roberts's Reflected Best-Self Exercise had a big effect on me and my own research. They are at the very core of becoming exceptional.

I've spent a long time working on a new approach, called the positive method, that integrates Seligman's and Roberts's research. Once you understand how the positive method can change the way your mind works, we're going to use it to create your own personal highlight reel.

Your highlight reel allows you to relive the moments when you were closest to your full potential, which will improve your mental well-being and help you reach your dreams and goals. But the point is not only to bathe in the success that comes from this process. In recognizing your most exceptional qualities and strengths, the positive method ultimately helps you make your best impact in the world around you and in the lives of those you care for the most. Using your strengths to make a positive influence on others is what creates real satisfaction with life, long after the buzz of awards—and financial rewards—fades away.

This is where it gets exciting, because there is much more power in positive psychology than just feeling nice. When we experience positive psychology, our brain operates differently, and we are able to create better outcomes in the world—for example, positive psychology allows us to find more creative solutions to problems and improves our physical health. The next few sections will give you a glimpse into the surprising science behind positivity and our brains.

HOW POSITIVITY UNLOCKS YOUR BRAIN'S POTENTIAL

In a study conducted by Janine Dutcher, a psychology professor at UCLA, she hooked people up to fMRIs, which are machines that measure brain activity. Dutcher had half of the subjects write about an everyday item (like a toaster). The other half she asked to write about their unique values. The people who reflected on unique values triggered a part of the brain called the "seeking system."

And when the seeking system is activated, it releases dopamine—a neurotransmitter linked to motivation and pleasure.

Dopamine is what our body produces to make us feel enthusiastic, excited, and stimulated to do more.

Emotions like enthusiasm and excitement feel good, but they also make us more creative and help us make better decisions. Back in the 1990s, American psychologists Alice Isen, Martin Seligman, and Barbara Fredrickson rocked the world of psychology by revealing that our positive emotions help us tap into our brain's potential. Three decades later, evidence continues to roll in: positive emotions improve our mental functioning. Threat, anxiety, and fear—while great for fight or flight—narrow our perceptions and diminish creative problem-solving.

Imagine, for example, that you signed up for a creativity task in a lab at Harvard University. You go into a room and on a table there is a candle, a book of matches, and a box with ten thumbtacks in it. You have three minutes to attach the lit candle to the wall.

So, how would you do it?

One solution that does work is to dump out the thumbtacks, pin the box to the wall, and use it as a candleholder. This solution requires creativity and nonlinear thinking, because you need to reframe the box in your mind as performing a new function.

This was a study I worked on with Julia Lee, a management professor teaching at the University of Michigan, and Fran Gino, a Harvard Business School professor. In a control group, subjects tried to solve this problem before reading highlight reel stories written about them by family and friends. In this control group, only 19% of people were able to see this solution and solve the problem. A second group was assigned to read their highlight reel stories before attempting the task, and 51% of this group solved the candle problem. How is it even possible that people became over twice as likely to solve the problem just by reading some stories about themselves?

Because during stressful times, positive emotions allow us to channel our cognitive resources. Positive emotions let us cope with the task at hand, instead of being bogged down by fear and threat. They open us up to information and new ways of thinking. This is why doctors make much more accurate diagnoses, and salespeople make more sales, when they experience positive emotions (instead of feeling neutral or negative emotions).

So you see, activating our positive psychology with highlight reels does more than just feel good. It also improves our creativity and helps us make better decisions.

SHARING YOUR UNIQUE PERSPECTIVE

Your highlight reel focuses on what is unique about you, capturing the moments when you are using your own perspective and strengths. This focus encourages us to contribute our personal ideas and skills, leading to better teamwork.

Julia Lee, Fran Gino, and I examined these ideas in another study where we focused on 330 military cadets in the United States Air Force at Officer Training School. The cadets completed a Web-based simulation that allows five-person teams to make decisions in the face of challenges as they climb Mt. Everest. Different team members received different information. Like real life, the best team outcomes demand that team members share their unique knowledge. For example, in the medical challenge, the team cannot make a good decision (e.g., deciding not to proceed to the next camp and avoiding frostbite) if the environmentalist does not provide the team with a screenshot of the windchill chart to calculate the predicted temperature in the next camp.

All of the cadets in the study received a personal highlight reel, created by my company Essentic. However, half the teams received their highlight reel before starting the simulation, while the other half received them after the study was completed.

Team members who received their highlight reels ahead of time felt more affirmed and were significantly more likely to share their information and perspectives (compared to those who received their highlight reels after the study was completed). We confirmed our finding with 246 senior leaders attending a program at Harvard's

Kennedy School, participating in an immersive seven-day simulation. Teams that received their highlight reels before starting the simulation performed better than those who received their highlight reels after the study was completed.

When we feel affirmed by focusing on what we do well, we are more likely to improve our impact by sharing our unique perspectives and ideas.

BUILDING AUTHENTICITY AND RESILIENCE

In one of the interviews I conducted with a woman by the name of Samantha who had just finished reading her highlight reel, I discovered how happy it makes us when the people in our lives see us the same way we see ourselves. As Samantha put it, "I do not want to 'wear a mask on my face' and I try to be as genuine as possible. I am very glad that people see me the way I try to behave."

It feels good when we are authentic—when our external behaviors match our internal states. And across all my research and interviews, the data show that people feel more authentic after reading their personal highlight reels. We saw this in the study I described in the introduction with the data entry at Harvard and the replication study at Wipro in India.

Feeling authentic gives us a sense of contentment, but it also makes us more resilient. It helps us persist toward our goals and keeps us healthier in the face of stress. Why? Because it takes more energy to hide parts of ourselves than to live authentically. Psychologists like Alicia Grandey at the Pennsylvania State University call this "emotional labor." When we try to hide who we really are, it's like a form of uncompensated work. Grandey found that when employees felt they could be authentic they were less likely to "burn out" at work.

Julia Lee and our research team also tested whether personal highlight reels could help with resilience to stress and disease. We invited participants to a laboratory session. When they arrived, we seated them in cubicles and attached sensors to them to measure their anxiety. We also collected saliva from participants, so that we could measure their immunity. We gave half the people their highlight reels before the session, while the other half received their reels after the session. Then we put some stress on the participants, using a "CyberBall" simulation, where they felt ostracized from a group game of "digital catch."

Being ignored by the other players was frustrating for the participants. Imagine being excluded in a game for twenty passes in a row! Their faces went from amused to puzzled to frustrated. The skin sensors showed that all participants experienced an increase in stress while being excluded from the game, but individuals who received their highlight reels beforehand bounced right back from this stress, whereas the other half of the participants continued to be agitated and flustered. And get this: Individuals who received their highlight reels ahead of the experiment also experienced big increases in physical immunity compared to those who did not get their highlight reels.

Activating our best selves with a highlight reel increases our resilience against both social stress and sickness.

INCREASING YOUR SENSE OF PURPOSE

People feel life has a purpose when they view their lives as coherent, significant, and aligned with their values. Not surprisingly, then, many of us feel a heightened sense of purpose when we use our unique strengths to help our families, our friends, and our colleagues. We feel purposeful when do what we were born to do. It's a peak human feeling—one that we would ideally experience more often.

Your personal highlight reel can increase your sense of purpose. When other people notice and appreciate your strengths, it feels good and it reinforces those qualities. For example, after reading his highlight reel, a man named Mark told me, "Whether it was helping a friend who had been broken up with or helping someone study for a test, I never considered these moments worthy of praise. I had assumed these were always simple acts of friendship. But when reading these [stories], I felt a sense of love and purpose."

Your sense of purpose is more than just a feel-good emotion. It also affects your ability to inspire others. If you are a parent, you may wonder how you can inspire your children to pursue their potential. Well, think about it: It's very difficult to be an inspiring role model for your children if you don't feel you make a difference, or don't feel that life is very meaningful yourself. But your children definitely will notice if you wake up in the morning with a sense of meaning around your daily activities. Children notice how parents talk about their day. The same goes for teachers who want to inspire students to bring their best to school. And the same for leaders: It's hard to inspire others if you yourself are not inspired.

I hope that by showing you all this research, you are starting to see the connected loop between what you feel and how you act. When you experience positive emotions and become more creative, that creativity makes you feel more positive, which makes you more creative, and so on. This creates an upward spiral. The same happens when you feel more purpose: You inspire the people around you, and their inspiration charges you up and increases your sense of purpose even more, which inspires more people, and so on. The upward spiral is a virtuous circle. It is also a renewable resource.

Yet making your personal highlight reel is not always easy or comfortable. Why? I'll tell you all about it in the next chapter. As we saw with the Dela gratitude videos, social norms have made it difficult to learn about our peak moments. Our culture doesn't make it easy to confide in one another when we recognize each other's strengths. Our brains fool us into thinking there is plenty of time later for sharing our appreciation for others and for pursuing our best possible life. These social norms are *hidden forces* that push us back from our potential. Let's learn more about these hidden forces and how to overcome them.

CHAPTER 2

The Hidden Forces That Limit Us

D ave Maher, a bearded mid-thirties comedian and actor, had been hard on his body for many years. He was a problem drinker who didn't eat well and was constantly high. He was also a type 1 diabetic. After selling all his test strips to buy weed, Dave had no way of monitoring his blood sugar. One day his levels skyrocketed, his kidneys failed, and his body shut down. Dave had fallen into a coma.

Three weeks later, the doctors didn't think that Dave would come through and told Dave's family it was probably better to take him off life support. Dave's mother and father, distraught and beaten down, invited his friends to the hospital room to say their goodbyes.

Blake, a good friend of Dave's, couldn't bring himself to go to the hospital when he learned they were going to remove the life support. When later asked in an interview, Blake said there was no way he could see Dave like that, knowing that he'd never be able to talk to him again.

After saying their goodbyes, Dave's friends had left the hospital assuming his family would pull the plug sometime during the night. The next day, the Facebook post that Blake dreaded came in. "Rest in Peace Dave Maher." Overwhelmed with sadness and memories, Blake sat stunned. After a while, he wrote, "I love you dude" on Dave's wall, along with a treasured memory of Dave. Basically, he had posted a digital eulogy. When asked if he had ever told Dave that to his face, Blake said, "I don't think so. When you're faced with actually losing them, you realize it more. Unfortunately that's how it works."

As it turned out, lots of other people did the same thing. In total, Dave's friends posted about a hundred eulogies for him on social media. Two weeks after this outpouring, a post came from Dave's Facebook page: "This is Dave Maher. Spoiler alert: I'm here."

It was Thanksgiving Day. But Dave turned it into Easter.

His parents never did wind up taking him off life support—it had only been a rumor. They had actually transferred him to a different hospital instead. Then one day his dad walked in and starting talking to him and Dave's eyes popped open. He had a whole mess of tubes coming out of his face, but he could still mouth the words "What the *fuck*?!"

Dave had been in a coma for a month.

It took another month for Dave to come out of the hospital. One night after he had been released, he settled in with his laptop at the little kitchen island in his parents' basement, and he started reading all of those eulogies.

Dave got to see what he looked like, from the outside. The stories rang truest to him when they highlighted his slanted, oblique view on life that often made others laugh. But the more Dave considered his friends' stories, the more he felt some disconnect between his version of himself and theirs.

In an interview recounting these events on *This American Life*, Dave's voice broke with tears when he described the eulogies his friends had posted: "So many of these things I didn't even remember. I don't remember things that way."

Some of the stories that surprised him the most were ones that showed he was the kind of guy who came through for the people in his life. A friend named Duffer described how Dave treated him as an equal in college, even though Dave was a senior while he was a freshman. He wrote, "Thanks for telling me not to be so hard on myself, and then laughing about how funny that sounded coming from you. Thanks for all the rides home. Thanks for being my best friend."

For much of his life, Dave had thought of himself, essentially, as a bad person. At his core, he saw himself as insensitive and self-centered. But the stories from his friends were the equivalent of Dave's *highlight reel*, showing him what others valued most about him, from his sense of humor to his loyalty to his friendships. This was how they saw him when he was at his best. The stories taught Dave that he was so much more than he thought to the people he cared about. Dave's sense of self was expanded by what he read.

How is it that we often don't know what makes us special or where we are exceptional until we hear it from other people? That is one of the mysteries that this book will help unravel.

Dave got to hear his own eulogy. He saw his unique strengths through the eyes of those who have known and valued him over the years.

Lucky bastard.

It might sound strange to call Dave lucky, given what he went through, but his experience changed his life in an incredible way. Both the journey of getting close to death and the positive jolt of hearing his own eulogy caused Dave to shift cognitive gears and transform his perspective of himself. Dave's experience allowed him to break through the two hidden forces that hold us all back from recognizing our potential.

THE FIRST HIDDEN FORCE

I call the first hidden force the *eulogy delay*—the cultural resistance to appreciating people's unique strengths until after they have passed away. Much of the time we don't *tell* other people what we appreciate most about them, and we don't *ask* other people what they appreciate most about us. The eulogy delay makes it feel unacceptable to call attention to positive behaviors and qualities in ourselves and others.

Once the person dies, then the phobia clears up, and the eulogy delay ends. It then becomes culturally acceptable to share those thoughts and memories. Of course, it is *possible* to share this information with each other now, while we are still alive.

Let me introduce you to twenty-one-year-old Ron, a journalism student at the University of Michigan who took a class on positive psychology. As part of this class, one of the assignments was Laura Morgan Roberts's Reflected Best-Self Exercise: Reach out to family and friends and ask them to send you memories of you at your best. Ron felt like this was a really strange ask. He had never given or received—or asked for—this type of feedback in his life. He found the assignment very awkward and almost dropped the class. Ron was experiencing the eulogy delay.

At the time, Ron told his girlfriend Carla, "I'm not sure I can ask my parents and my Detroit high school buddies to rave about me. They'll think I lost it." But Carla recommended he try it. She reminded him that the only way you ever learned something in life was when you tried something new. Carla's wisdom prevailed, Ron beat back his phobia, and he reached out to family, friends, and teachers for their memories of him.

When he read the stories his network sent, Ron was floored. Within a few minutes of starting to read, he found tears running down his cheeks. He said, "I was in utter shock. I had no idea that my friends and family felt so passionately for me." By the time he'd finished, he said, "I was completely bawling." His father's story was the one that really choked him up, as Ron explained:

> My dad isn't around that much, and he is not an emotional man whatsoever. He wrote me a fairly long story detailing my quest for knowledge and my ability to understand others. I truly never knew my dad felt this way about me, because he has never told me in person.

Ron said his highlight reel made him feel genuinely proud of himself and empowered in a way that he was not used to. Here's how Ron put it: "I never knew how much I was loved and appreciated, because I spend most of my time putting myself down."

The eulogy delay is maddening because it holds us back from recognizing what we are capable of, which often takes an outsider's perspective. Like we saw with Ron and Dave, our network, the people who know us best, are able to see and value our unique gifts in ways we simply can't from the driver's seat. Their perspective can help us validate the qualities we recognize in ourselves. More importantly, they can pinpoint strengths that are completely outside our personal narratives and show us our positive blind spots.

As we will see in the next chapter, study after scientific study make it clear that the stories we use to describe ourselves affect the way we act. If you can improve your personal narrative, you can improve your behaviors. But the hidden force of the eulogy delay holds us back from seeing our full potential, so we are instead left focusing on stories about our limitations.

The eulogy delay is also frustrating because it deters us from deepening our relationships, making us feel awkward when we help others understand what we value most about them. Yet the science shows that the best way to improve our social relationships is to share our appreciation for others. And when it comes to enjoying life, studies show good social relations are *necessary* for happiness and for living a long, healthy life. That's right: If you are not working toward strong social relationships, it's as dangerous as smoking cigarettes. And not having good relationships creates a *greater* risk of early death than alcohol consumption, obesity, and air pollution.

Luckily, there are ways to overcome this invisible boundary that exists between us and those around us. In chapter 5, we'll look deeper into the genesis of the eulogy delay and find ways to beat it.

THE SECOND HIDDEN FORCE

The second hidden force that Dave broke through when he heard his own eulogy is what I call *transience aversion*. It refers to our resistance to thinking about our mortality. It is that gut-level discomfort we feel when we remember that we will not live forever. The science shows that most people try to keep this truth far away from their minds. Even reading this now, you might be experiencing a bit of transience aversion. Sorry about that. We humans just do not like to be reminded that our lives will end someday.

Of course, on one level, we *know* that we're mortal. But day-to-day we live as if death is optional, a far-off concept. I was doing that myself before I got my cancer wake-up call. I had trouble admitting it, but before I was diagnosed I was acting like I had unlimited time instead of pursuing my dreams. Because of transience aversion, many of us find ourselves treating our life as a dress rehearsal.

But our subconscious knows when we are idling, and a part of us dwindles as our potential curdles inside us. Because of this, many of us end up with what is called "existential regret"—the sense of having abandoned and betrayed our self, of forfeiting our own potential. It is that feeling we get when we know we could have done more, or when we lived inauthentically.

Dave's experience helped him break through this second hidden force. He suddenly saw how short life can be and how unexpectedly we can run out of time to pursue the life we truly want. Dave began to live a better version of his self:

I am sober; fully recovered physically; in a healthy, adult relationship with a woman I love; and a more responsible person and productive comedian than ever before. By all accounts, I'm thriving.

This brings to mind the story of Alfred Nobel, who you might know as the benefactor of some of the most prestigious awards for human achievement. Originally, however, Nobel was famous for developing explosives. He invented dynamite and racked up 355 patents for nitroglycerine detonators, blasting caps, and smokeless gunpowder. Nobel became wealthy from his inventions, and he owned nearly one hundred factories that made explosives and munitions.

I know what you're thinking: "What makes a person change from weapons tycoon to world benefactor?" How did the "explosives king" end up investing his vast estate into efforts of peace, literature, medicine, chemistry, and physics?

Maybe it was because he accepted his life as transient.

In 1888, Nobel's brother Ludvig died in France from a heart attack. Apparently, a French newspaper reporter believed that it was Alfred who had died, and wrote an obituary focused on him growing wealthy as a "merchant of war." So Alfred experienced his own death in writing, jolting him into re-evaluating his life. Perhaps he realized he was working for his resume rather than his eulogy and the impact he was making. In any case, Nobel became obsessed with changing the world for the better with the fortune he had amassed.

This is why transience aversion is the second hidden force we need to beat, because remembering we will not be here on earth for long can help us align our lives with our values. It gives us the urgency to pursue our potential.

The eulogy delay and transience aversion are hidden forces because they *feel* natural. It feels "natural" to avoid the vulnerability of expressing our full appreciation of others, just as we "naturally" push back thoughts of our own lives ending. This book is all about breaking through these obstacles, because when we are lucky enough to do so, we start living fuller lives. Your personal highlight reel is key to making this happen.

Over the last ten years I have been studying and conducting empirical research on the effects of highlight reels. My research colleagues and I collected qualitative data from students in positive psychology classes who had gone through the process, giving us insights into people just starting out their careers. And, on the other end of the spectrum, we interviewed partners from a global consulting firm.

We discovered similar findings emerging from younger people and older people, from men and women, and from people all around the world. Across almost every case, the highlight reel experience helped people break through the eulogy delay and transience aversion.

In the next few sections you will discover just how powerful and life-altering it was for them to free themselves of these forces.

HOW LIVING EULOGIES CHANGE OUR LIVES

Let's go back to Dave's experience. Something held Dave's friends back from telling him what he meant to them, until they thought he was gone. They unintentionally hid their poignant stories about times he had improved their lives. Some of those memories occurred *decades* prior to Dave's coma, going back to college and before. But the eulogy delay made his friends hold their appreciation in.

Subsequently, Dave didn't realize the positive ways he affected the people around him. His impression of himself focused on his negative traits, like his insensitivity. Focusing on his faults reduced Dave's self-esteem and made his life difficult and often painful.

Unfortunately, many of us tend to go through life focused on the negative side. While certainly it can be useful to be aware of both sides, focusing on our weaknesses is not very motivating. It can make life harder to navigate and enjoy.

When we hear how we are valued by other people it can improve the way we see ourselves. And sometimes, the very traits we beat ourselves up over turn out to be traits that other people admire the most. For example, before reading his highlight reel, Michigan student Ron, who you met a little earlier, had seen his careful planning as a flaw:

> *Although I know of my organizational capabilities, and how they help me to complete tasks, I tend to view this trait negatively. I sometimes feel as though my need to create an*

agenda for each day hinders spontaneity and impacts times of exploration and discovery.

This is so insightful, because it shows how we all have strengths and weaknesses. In fact, sometimes they are just the flip side of each other. People who are very organized also restrict spontaneity, but that doesn't mean we can't appreciate this quality.

By breaking through the eulogy delay and completing his highlight reel, Ron was able to transform what he believed was a limitation into a valued part of who he is. He recognized that across his network, people gave consistent feedback of how much they treasured his organizational skills:

Hearing that my meticulous and thoughtful schedules are appreciated and valued relieves this internal conflict. My intent in every situation is to make others feel important, and to know they recognize this constant effort of mine gives a new sense of meaning to my daily routines.

Overcoming this hidden force, and experiencing our own living eulogy, can help us find self-acceptance and healing. It can give us the courage to live authentically, and in many ways it can inspire us to offer up the best possible version of ourselves to the people we love.

Meet Tracey, an actress and a young economics major in the same class as Ron. Like many of us, Tracey often focused on her weaknesses. In her words: "I tend to beat myself up a lot, and I believe that I am selfish. I have this complex where I feel as if I am never doing enough for other people."

When she initially heard she would be asking family and friends for memories of her at her best, Tracey was skeptical. Due to the eulogy delay, it felt greedy and egocentric to her to ask for only positive feedback. She was swayed when her professor discussed the exercise as a way to improve her relationships and her contributions to other people.

This was an important mental shift—instead of thinking about the exercise as *tell me how great I am,* Tracey started thinking about it as *help me learn how to make my best impact on others.*

So, she pushed through the awkward feelings and focused on how the highlight reel could strengthen her connections to those she cared about:

> *Most all of my stories spoke to my compassionate nature: helping my sister when she wet her pants in kindergarten, driving my friend to class when her ride was late, and personally greeting everyone who comes to see me in my plays at the stage door. These stories taught me that while I am busy criticizing myself for being "selfish," my loved ones never cease to notice all my little kind acts of compassion; that makes me feel very confident in myself.*

It can be game-changing to learn how our best self is seen by others. When was the last time *you* shared a memory with someone to help them understand who they are at their best? In chapter 5, we're going to reach out to people we care about—friends, family, and colleagues—and share some of our memories with them. Because we don't have that much time, and we don't have to wait.

PUSHING THROUGH THE RESISTANCE

Through Essentic, I've helped create highlight reels for tens of thousands of people. And one thing I've learned is that many people initially resist approaching their social network for highlights—almost like it is illegal or unethical. And then, once we give people their highlight reels, they sometimes hesitate to read them or feel a sense of discomfort.

This discomfort is due to the eulogy delay. We don't often practice communicating or focusing on strengths. The result is that it can feel awkward, at first, to ask for, and even receive, appreciation. Tracey felt this tension before reading her highlight reel for the first time:

It felt like a new kind of vulnerability, because I would be seeing myself not through my own eyes, but through the lens of some of the people that I am closest to. I knew that all of the stories would be positive reflections of my identity and personality, yet I was nervous to gain insight on how my friends and family perceived my actions and who I was.

Yet, *after* reading their stories, people's resistance melts away. In fact, once they have broken through the eulogy delay, people are very thankful for the push. As Tracey said, "Once I began reading the stories, my heart began to fill with warmth. Not only did I feel an immense amount of love and appreciation for those who wrote me stories, but I felt a great deal of honor and pride in myself."

In the beginning, Tom, a fifty-two-year-old partner in a consulting firm in Chicago, also felt resistance to the process. When Tom first heard he was going to create a personal highlight reel, four years ago, he was a little skeptical and felt that he was doing something almost culturally taboo. I asked Tom to describe his initial reaction to the highlight reel process:

You don't ask people for feedback generally, but then the concept that it would be only positive feedback was certainly not something that I'd ever done. "Yeah, instead of talking about politics or whatever over dinner, let's all just reflect upon what we value from one another." That conversation just doesn't happen.

However, Tom was taking part in an executive program at London Business School at the time, and part of the program was creating his highlight reel. So, Tom broke through the eulogy delay and went for it. He was surprised by what he discovered about himself. As he put it, "You don't always know the depth and appreciation there is for things you're doing. Not necessarily big things you're doing, but everyday things you're doing—and how others are impacted."

This theme is something I hear again and again when I talk with people who have created their highlight reels. They are often very touched when people reflect on the small things they've done over the course of their lives. It's a little like the movie *It's A Wonderful Life*—we often forget that our small, daily actions are valued by other people. As Tom put it, "We get so absorbed in our own day-to-day lives that we don't really step back to appreciate how we are impacting others."

Tom told me that the stories that affected him the most were from his sixteen-year-old daughter Lina, who has epilepsy. Lina shared some memories of when she was going through health issues, and she described how Tom helped her to grow and make it through some very difficult days. Four years later, Tom told me, "I still think about those stories all the time."

Take a moment now to think about the force that is preventing *you* from helping others recognize what makes them special. You might find that it's pretty odd when you examine it objectively. We carry these treasured memories around, sometimes for decades. We move them forward in our mental drawers, even while we forget so many other things. Why would we cart these stories around of other people, but not reveal them until after they die?

What a flawed approach to living.

Here's the thing: Each of our personalities has a valuable bright side and a thornier shadow side. But we tend to concentrate on the thorns. We focus on what we can improve. Think about New Year's resolutions. We usually focus on weaknesses to exorcise or bad habits to break, rather than doing more of what we do best.

This is how we treat other people too. We let them know when they've made us angry. But we rarely tell them about the times they make us bigger, better, happier. However, if you focus on "fixing" their limitations, you may be eliminating exactly what is most special about them.

It's like a little island that doesn't have an airport, but is incredibly unique because it is so remote. It can be a real pain to get there, but the inaccessibility is also part of its beauty. If you fix this limitation and add an airport, soon the island gets crowded, and you lose what made it special in the first place.

When Dave read his friends' eulogies, he saw that they accepted and even appreciated the thornier aspects of his personality. Their stories showed how his interpersonal intensity and combativeness were actually part of what they cherished about him. Dave said, "Here, I had concrete, digital evidence that I was understood to the core of my personality. I found myself thinking, *I'm actually a pretty good dude. I did life right.*"

This is one of the most valuable things about highlight reels. They allow us to share, and see, positive strengths rather than focusing on limitations.

Ron put it like this: "Gaining this new understanding of my influence on the people in my life made me feel treasured, admired, and understood. These are feelings that I had never experienced before in this capacity, but that I believe every person should get the chance to feel."

Now it's time to make these ideas personal, with an exercise that combines what you've learned about each hidden force. Trigger warning! This exercise could make you uncomfortable, but that's the point—you need to push past that resistance. Now that you understand how important our living eulogies are, it's time to start creating your own. Remember, you are not working for your resume here. You are working for a well-lived life in which you can feel fulfilled.

★ *Break Down the Hidden Forces* ★

If you were able to hear your own eulogy, what would you want people to say? On a blank piece of paper or in an online document, write down what you hope they would say about you. To get you started, take fifteen minutes to reflect on these questions, and jot down your ideas.

- What did you stand for?

- What did you do best?

- What did you contribute that was unique?

- How did you make people feel?

Now, create a folder—digital or physical—that will become your personal highlight reel over the course of reading this book. Add your thoughts about your eulogy to your personal highlight reel folder. We'll do many more exercises as we progress through this book. Each time, you can add the output to your highlight reel. In addition to our exercises together, some people fill their folder with photos of their happiest memories, achievements, and dreams for inspiration and encouragement. It helps you remember the goals, principles, and ideals you'd like to live your life by.

Okay, so now you know more about the eulogy delay and how we resist sharing strengths and unique contributions with each other. Now, let's turn to understanding that second hidden force a bit better.

WHAT HAPPENS WHEN WE EMBRACE OUR MORTALITY

No one likes to think about death. That's natural. We don't like to think about the end, so most of us just don't. It's why most adults still haven't arranged a will even late into their golden years, despite the mess they leave behind for their families.

But it's useful to be aware of our impermanence. When we acknowledge our fragility, we can make better plans about how to live. Being jolted into thinking about our obituary, like Alfred Nobel, reminds us that we still have time to use our unique strengths to make a difference. If we can break through the force of transience aversion, and be mindful about our mortality, we become more engaged in life.

Recognizing how delicate our lives are can help us appreciate our day-to-day more. It causes us to savor the small moments—a sunset or holding a daughter's hand—and to experience more fulfillment and gratitude every day.

It may sound ironic, but many people who survive near-death experiences—from car crashes to cancer to comas—end up getting more living out of life than before their trauma. They begin doing what they always knew they could be doing with their life, but hadn't gotten around to. This is known as *post-traumatic growth*.

This is how Dave broke through both the eulogy delay and transience aversion. His coma gave him the rare chance to attend his own funeral—à la Tom Sawyer. His trusted friends described him at his best. These insights inspired Dave, comforted him, and expanded his understanding of himself. Dave also grasped, firsthand, how death can come at any time. This motivated him to focus on improving his relationships, his health, and his comedy while he still had the time.

Breaking free of the hidden forces is allowing Dave to become exceptional. By exceptional, I don't mean that Dave will ever be perfect. I don't mean he has become the best comedian in the world, or the finest of all friends. What I mean is that Dave is getting closer to his own potential. He is becoming his own version of exceptional, more often.

Do we have to almost die to experience the benefits of accepting transience? As we'll see in chapter 4, the benefits of post-traumatic growth don't come from the *physical* threat. The energy to change comes from any jolt or event that causes you to question your assumptions about life. And the best part is it can come from a hugely positive event in your life. This is exactly what your highlight reel is designed to do.

Our highlight reels are positive transformational events that help us live beyond these forces. They are events that allows us to reinvent the stories we tell ourselves about who we are and our lives. In the next chapter, we will look at those stories and see how improving your personal narrative can help you access what makes you exceptional.

CHAPTER 3

Possible Selves

"Our tales are spun, but for the most part,
we don't spin them; they spin us."

—DANIEL DENNETT

Think about the last piece of clothing you bought. Was it a crisp white shirt? Bright colored socks? Or perhaps some camo running shoes?!

In any case, you picked something that sends a message about you. That's because we human beings are *self-aware*—we have a sense of who we are. When we choose to buy a tweed jacket or a pair of pre-ripped jeans, we want other people to know who we think we are.

This seems to be a key difference between human beings and other animals. I'm talking here about our high degree of self-awareness, not buying pre-ripped jeans. Over the last fifty thousand years, we humans *evolved very flexible brains that like to create stories about how we fit into the world.* We develop stories about the right way to live, and why we are here, and who made us.

But our most important story is the one we tell about ourselves. My story about what makes me *me*, and your story about what makes you *you*.

One of my primary goals in this book is to help you understand how your "self" is just a story. I know that sounds strange. In fact, many of us feel like our selves are a "real thing"—not "stories," but instead something objective and established, something that we just have to deal with.

The science in this chapter offers a very different perspective, because it helps us see that the self is a story. And, when you understand this, it allows you to edit, and change, your narrative. Ultimately, this is why your personal highlight reel will be so valuable to you—it reveals the version of you that is exceptional and helps you transform the way you see yourself.

It's powerful to think of the self as dynamic and not a fixed thing you are born with, because it means we can change who we are. You can't change where you were born, because that is fixed. The same with the year you were born: also fixed. You can lie about it, of course, but it doesn't change how old you are.

But our selves are malleable. We don't just receive who we are at birth, like we receive our genetics. No, our selves are stories that we develop.

Consider a six-year-old, whose only job is to experiment with the world and learn. As kids learn, they make mistakes. They try things and break things and get into trouble. It might be annoying to us parents, but trying things is how kids grow.

What happens if a kid's parents tell her that she's stupid whenever she makes mistakes? What if every time the child is trying something new, the parents shout, "You're an idiot" and "You always mess things up"? This is what it was like for Aileen growing up. As an only child of a very critical mother, Aileen received mostly negative feedback in her childhood.

Of course, Aileen is not an idiot—she had many positive traits and was just learning, like every kid does. But over time, what was the story that came to Aileen's mind about who she is? An undesirable story about someone who fails, who messes things up, who is not worthwhile. As a young adult, you could say that Aileen had developed and internalized a negative narrative about herself. Aileen described her relationship to her mother like this: "Her constant criticism and putting me down made me feel terrible about myself, and it made me double my efforts to please her . . . I was probably thirty before I realized there was nothing normal about how she talked to me."

Here is the kicker: Even when they are not true, the stories we tell ourselves about who we are have a way of becoming true.

As Aileen's story about herself became increasingly negative, it affected the way she interpreted the world, which in turn changed her reactions and decisions in the world. For example, instead of persevering when she experiences a setback, she's more likely to think, "I failed because I'm too stupid and worthless to do anything else." As a result, Aileen will be less likely to try new activities and take on new challenges, or learn to develop her strengths. She'll be less confident when she meets new people, so they won't respond to her as favorably as they could have. When she is dating, she'll be more likely to choose someone who treats her badly, because it feels natural or like what she thinks she deserves.

The stories we adopt about ourselves affect our behaviors. If you can change the story, then you can change your life.

THE MANY-FACETED SELF

Who I am on a Berlin weekend getaway with an old friend might seem like a different self from who I am when having dinner with my family, but, of course, both are me. A soldier at home is often different from that same person during combat. We have many *different* selves, not a single, immovable self.

The most current scientific research views the self as many-faceted ideas about who we are. Different elements of our self can be activated, or "working," depending on the situation and our own intentions. As one of your selves is activated and directing your behaviors, the others are subdued.

So, who are *you*? Here's a short exercise to get you thinking about your various selves and identities. On a piece of paper, a document on your computer, or in the lines on the left-hand column, write in the different answers that come to mind when you reflect on the question "Who am I?" You can think of the various roles that you play in life (for example, I am a dad, a husband, a professor, and a friend), and you also can think about the type of person you are in those various roles (for example, I'm playful, goal-oriented, curious, and extroverted). We'll come back to the second column shortly; for now, focus on answering "Who am I?"

"Who am I?"   *"Who might I become?"*

_____   _____
_____   _____
_____   _____
_____   _____
_____   _____

YOUR POSSIBLE SELF

Have you ever seen someone living their life in ways that you wish you could replicate? When we see people running marathons, traveling the world, shining with confidence, earning a big promotion, or doing the things we dream of accomplishing, we think, "I could become like them." We then begin crafting our lives to be more like that image of our future possible self. When you buy those ripped jeans at the store, after all, it is your *future* self who will be wearing them.

As you can see, our knowledge about our self is bigger and broader than who we are *now*. It includes the selves of the past, the present, and possible selves we could become in the future. Our possible selves are made up of both who we would like to become and who we are afraid of someday becoming. Possible selves that we hope for might include the successful self, the creative self, the rich self, or the loved self. Our dreaded possible selves could be the alone self, the unhealthy self, or the unemployed self.

Now go back to the second column in the exercise marked "Who might I become?" and write in some of your possible selves. What is an ideal self that you might strive to become? What are some selves that you worry about becoming someday, if you are not careful? Don't worry; writing down your fears won't make them true. In fact, articulating them can help you find ways to avoid them!

These exercises are just ways of starting to reveal what's going on inside your brain. As we will see later in this chapter, the way that your brain stores and accesses your ideas about who you are affects how you act and respond to situations.

When you are finished with the "Who am I?" and "Who might I become?" exercise, take a picture, rip the page out, or take the piece of paper and put it in your highlight reel folder. This will help you remember throughout this process where you are coming from and who you are striving to be.

THE STORY WE TELL OURSELVES

Let me introduce you to some research that shows how we can edit our personal stories, which changes our behaviors, which affects the results we create in the world. The study focuses on high school students in Detroit.

In the United States, the national average for on-time graduation is 75%. But it is only 50% for African Americans and 53% for Hispanics. In Detroit, graduation estimates hover around 40%. Daphna Oyserman and her colleagues at the University of Michigan thought these low graduation rates could have something to do with students' possible selves—the people they hoped to become, and feared becoming, in the future.

Because get this: Society floods us with stories of low achievement when it comes to low-income minority youth. According to research published in *Sociological Forum*, high school students— even Latino and African American students—perceive Latinos as more likely to become manual laborers and expect African Americans to do poorly in school. In low-income neighborhoods, kids see a lot of adults with low academic attainment and nonprofessional jobs. Naturally, manual labor can be meaningful work, but many high school students' dreams are unnecessarily limited because they believe that this, or unemployment, is their only possible future.

So when low-income Latinos or African Americans imagine themselves in the future, what jumps to their minds are often limiting stories. These narrow or negative possible selves are highly accessible in their brains. In fact, as Oyserman notes, if low-income Latinos or African Americans need to ask for help from the teacher (a good habit for an academic self), they often feel they are contradicting their racial identity (asking a teacher for help is "such a white thing to do"). When their possible "high achievement in school" self *conflicts* with their other identities, it is easier to imagine being the sort of person who gets low grades, and even quits school.

So, Oyserman and her colleagues got involved. They designed an intervention where they helped low-income eighth graders in Detroit middle schools develop academic selves. The experiment consisted of eleven sessions for students during their homeroom period. The sessions were about one hour each. As a control, a second group of students just attended regular homeroom sessions.

Here are some specific examples of the interventions. In the first session, the kids talked in groups and then each introduced another student in terms of the skills that student possessed that would help him or her complete the school year successfully. "This is Manuel, and he is very organized and has a positive attitude." In session 2, students picked photographs that fit their adult "visions" of themselves and described their success in their own words. In sessions 3 and 4, students drew role models that provided motivation as they worked toward their possible selves, and also drew the people who were draining their energy.

In sessions 5, 6, and 7, students represented the behaviors that go with their academic selves, using art to express this, including poster boards, stickers, and markers. Sessions 8, 9, and 10 focused on social problems, academic problems, and the process of getting to high school graduation. The final session was a review.

In total, each student put in around twelve hours, across seven weeks, editing their stories. What do you think? Could these brief sessions, which helped students develop academic selves, really change anything?

First off, the data revealed that the intervention indeed affected students' possible selves, which affected how students acted over the following year (while the control group did not change). They were absent from school two days less than those in the control group, earned significantly higher GPAs, and received higher standardized test scores. And more than *twice* as many kids in the control group dropped out compared to those in the intervention.

Do you remember in chapter 1 we talked about "upward spirals"? Well, Oyserman's intervention created an upward spiral resulting in long-term effects. Almost *two years* after the intervention, kids who developed academic selves were still spending significantly more time per week doing homework. These students also were significantly less disruptive in the classroom than those in the control group (for example, less likely to interfere with peers' work or be verbally abusive to teachers). These students showed more initiative and were more likely to do extra work and persist on difficult problems. Across time, the positive differences in grades became even *larger* between students with "academic possible selves" and those in the control group.

What does this study tell us? It simply is not accurate to think about ourselves as fixed. Oyserman's study shows how our possible selves can be crafted and developed, and how our behaviors and results follow those narratives. Without the intervention, these same kids were more likely to tell themselves stories that included skipping class, earning low grades, and dropping out. Instead, they became substantially more likely to succeed.

YOUR WORKING SELF

What's the first thing that comes to mind when you read the words "Coca-Cola"? What color do you think of? Is there a certain holiday that you are reminded of? Maybe you just think of sugar.

Coca-Cola has spent a lot of money on advertisements to make you think about the color *red*, the *Christmas* holiday, and the adjective *refreshing*.

Notice that the thoughts that first come to mind need not be true. As a liquid, Coca-Cola is not red. And of course Coca-Cola doesn't own any of the holidays. But when you think about Coca-Cola, something is happening in your mind to make some ideas *chronically accessible*. They seem to be at the top of our minds, so they jump into our thoughts quickly when prompted. So effortlessly, in fact, that we often don't even take time to question them or how they got there.

How did we get mentally hijacked? What's going on in our brains?

Most cognitive scientists accept *associative models* of memory, which are made up of nodes and linkages. Nodes are where our brains store information. The storage nodes are connected by neural linkages that are stronger or weaker depending on how often we use them.

One node (such as "Coca-Cola") becomes a source of activation for other nodes (such as "red" or "refreshing") when stored information is being retrieved from memory. Scientists call this "spreading activation." It's how we can access ideas from memory.

Why do some concepts (like *red* and *refreshing*) spring forth from our memory quicker than others? Because in the end, a brain works just like a muscle. I know it doesn't feel that way to many people. In fact, for most of human history we didn't see brains that way. Until pretty recently, people thought that the number of brain connections and neurons was finite. People thought the physical adult brain was unchangeable.

But in the last thirty years, technology has helped neuroscience make great progress. And the science shows us that the brain can change quite a bit because it works like a muscle. For example, when you try to do pull-ups, you make your biceps bigger and stronger and you can do more pull-ups. When you consistently pair one concept (Coca-Cola) with another concept (red), your brain makes the connection between the concepts stronger. So when you think Coca-Cola, red comes to mind faster.

Forget about Coke for a minute. What adjectives jump to your mind first when you think about yourself? What story about yourself have you rehearsed the most? This is what psychologists call your "working self-concept."

★ *Uncover Your Working Self-Concept* ★

Take ten minutes to write down the first words that come to mind when you think about yourself. Write down whatever initially pops in your head, including adjectives that describe you, what makes you unique, and how you think you seem to other people. Of course, some of this may overlap with the possible selves you wrote about earlier. See what else jumps to mind.

When you are finished, add this exercise to your highlight reel folder. It's possible that some of this information will make you proud, and excited, and you'll want to keep it. It's possible that you will be ashamed of certain elements, such that you want to edit the story once you've completed your personal highlight reel. When you learn from other people how they experience you at your best, you will feel empowered to make that change.

FROM STORIES TO REALITY

The ideas emerging from the exercises in this chapter offer a mind map of how you see yourself. What came to mind fastest and naturally? This may be what you wrote down first. The answer matters, because the story that comes to mind quickest, your working self, is the one that most affects your behaviors and performance. This story about yourself affects your impact in the world.

Your goal is to edit your story so that the first thing it does is reflect your best self—not only because life feels better when you focus on your strengths, but also because you will improve your daily impact.

This might remind you of the popular self-help concept "positive visualization." But I'm not being all mystical here. We do not magically create "cosmic ordering" when we envision better results and positive stories—we still need to work hard for them. I'm not saying that wishful thinking makes the universe align with your personal wish list.

I'm saying that mental simulations of your best possible self prepare you to activate and enact that version of who you are. Like the imagery used by athletic superstars, it's how we turn ideas into action.

Achieving a desired outcome is more likely when you have a clear image of yourself in the future and a specific pathway for getting there. When we develop a personal highlight reel of concrete, specific examples that show what we are capable of, and practice being that more often, we rewire our brains to use this as our working self-concept. This makes us more likely to act that way in the future. It's basically making the best possible version of you more concrete, as we saw with Oyserman's study of inner-city students.

In part, this is due to the way our brains work (the strength of linkages). Some of this is also due to the fact that when we actively imagine events, it helps us plan behaviors and we gain more confidence that the events will actually occur. For example, alcoholics are less likely to relapse when they are instructed to imagine situations in which they might be tempted to drink, activate their sober self, and then rehearse how they will avoid giving in to that temptation.

Let me give you another example. Nicole Stephens, a management professor at Northwestern, conducted research on "first-generation" college students. Studies show that students whose parents didn't go to college are more likely to fail and drop out of university. The problem is not intellectual ability. The problem is the story they tell themselves about themselves. First-generation students often feel that they don't deserve to attend college, and they are especially likely to feel left out socially. We'll come back to the imposter syndrome in chapter 8.

Stephens and her colleagues helped a group of first-generation students develop a different narrative. They created a panel for them to learn how their class backgrounds can be both a challenge *and* a strength. Students learned how their different life experiences were valuable in classroom discussions (for example, helping other students build empathy). They learned that it was normal for them to rely on their advisers more than other students.

At the end of the first year of college, the GPA of most first-generation students was significantly below those students whose parents had attended college. However, for those students who developed a more productive story about their differences, there was no such "achievement gap."

Developing a different story about yourself is not magic. Real-world results come from hard work. In the study, students who developed a positive story about their social differences were more likely to meet with professors. They also were more likely to seek extra help from peers. And first-generation students with a more positive story not only *performed* better, but they also reported less anxiety and better adjustment to college, compared to first-generation students who did not develop a more productive story about themselves.

This is the secret to becoming your own version of exceptional: Change your "self story," change your habits, change your life. We all have strengths and limitations, and often they are two sides of the same coin. Which do you focus on? Personal highlight reels help us mentally rehearse our memories of peak performance, which strengthens the neural connections between our concept of self and our best behaviors.

TRANSFORM YOUR NEGATIVE SELF-TALK

We naturally do a lot of self-talk every single day, which is why it's important to stop and examine what kind of feedback we are giving ourselves.

Aileen's abusive mother focused on what Aileen did wrong, which caused Aileen to have negative self-talk ("I'm not good enough, I can't do this"), resulting in self-limiting behaviors (like not going to university and not applying for good jobs). Negative self-talk generally results in poor performance, resulting in a downward spiral. Personal highlight reels work because they give us a more productive story to tell ourselves by capturing what we do *right*. If you replace negative stories with thoughts centered on peak past performances, you can improve self-confidence and future performance.

To give you an example of how a highlight reel does this, let me introduce you to Antônia. From a very young age, learning and education were very important to her. When Antônia was six years old, her father worked all day in a veterinarian clinic in São Paulo, Brazil. In the evenings, he was working to complete his high school education at an adult school. Antônia remembers the following:

> *My father would get home late after school and he had his notebook, where he did the homework. And I remember that I liked that so much. I liked to sit with him when he was doing homework. I even remember his orange notebook with the bees building their nest. We would do the homework together. Of course I didn't understand anything, but I remember that I was proud, and that I wanted to be like him.*

Already at age twelve, Antônia knew she wanted to go to college in the United States. Of course, this was very unlikely, because she came from such a humble background. Her family was poor, and neither her mother nor her father had gone to college, nor had her older sister. But as Antônia said, "I knew I had to succeed because he was doing all that sacrifice. And when I was twelve, my father became a manager at the clinic where he worked. Then we were so happy. And that's how I am, I like when things take effort and when it's difficult, and then you get this reward."

So, Antônia worked very hard in high school and did well enough that she enrolled in a local university, where she obtained her undergraduate degree and a job as a consultant. Antônia said, "My employer had this sponsorship for people that performed well. And getting an MBA in the US became, for me, almost a dream. An obsession to go and study abroad." After a few years, she applied and was accepted to the University of Chicago, sponsored by her employer.

According to Antônia, her family cried when she was offered the MBA opportunity. She said, "They were so afraid that I would stay there in the US—'She's going to find something and she's going to leave us.'" But after her MBA, Antônia came back to São Paulo, to the company that sponsored her. A few years later, she accepted a different job with a more global consultancy. Over the years, she worked her way up to partner and then, most recently, managing director.

When I interviewed Antônia, she was two years into her managing director job, which was not yet going that well. We focused on her reactions to her highlight reel and what she learned from it:

My reaction was really very emotional, because I was in a moment when I was really questioning a lot. The work, my career and what I had achieved all those years until then was very important for me. And then I had two very difficult years at work, in terms of achieving my targets. So I was doubting myself. I was like, "Am I really that good? Did I reach a point where now I'm not competent or not a good professional?"

Even with all her accomplishments in her life and career, the destructive power of negative self-talk made Antônia question her abilities and self-worth. This is something that can easily lead to a downward spiral. Experiencing her highlight reel helped Antônia break that spiral, by allowing her to reflect on her core strengths instead of her weaknesses:

There was despair. Because I was doubting myself. I was like, "Who am I, what do I do?" I was kind of throwing my past away. Reading the stories was really emotional in the sense that, I saw I was good at something. And when I read that, I felt centered. I felt grounded.

Antônia's highlight reel reminded her of all the obstacles she had overcome, her determination and ability to persevere. It was a wake-up call to her potential when she needed it most.

As another example of how a highlight reel can change your self-talk, let's look at Ron from the previous chapter. Ron described how the stories from his highlight reel were helping him take control of the self-talk in his head in order to live a better life and also to use his strengths in his daily activities:

I've always had coaches, teachers, and family members that used deficit language to describe me—oftentimes bringing me down. Their language became the monologue in my head. For someone who struggles with self-doubt, this exercise made me realize, through the eyes of my loved ones, how I can truly be my best self.

This is one of the reasons why I, personally, am so motivated to teach and do research on highlight reels. By giving people the chance to participate in the positive method, I've witnessed how they become inspired when they understand the impact they can make with their unique strengths. I get to help them replace negative, defeating self-talk with positive emotions and narratives. And through their highlight reels they soon recognize that they are capable of activating their best possible selves—in fact, they realize they have already been this exceptional self many times throughout their lives. It's just a matter of getting there more often.

Do you remember the actress and engineering student Tracey from chapter 2? After experiencing her highlight reel, she said this:

Reading these stories lifted my spirits and gave me confidence in myself. I felt very in tune with who I aspired to be at my best, and how my friends and family saw me at my best. My initial reactions to these positive stories gave me the courage to believe in my strengths and abilities.

This is how highlight reels work. They let us rehearse concrete, specific memories about times we have used our strengths to make a real contribution. These stories affect how we think of ourselves, talk to ourselves, and motivate ourselves to become exceptional.

In this chapter, we saw how we need to be careful regarding which story about ourselves is most active, because we are listening—and our actions depend on it. We're going to make your best self *salient* and *accessible*, so that it is the first story that comes to mind. And the research shows that when your best self is activated, you'll be more likely to pursue goals and behaviors associated with that version of yourself.

Collecting and reflecting on your peak moments can lead to some powerful positive emotions, but the end goal is not only self-improvement or self-achievement. It's also about learning how to give more of ourselves to the world and to the relationships we value while we still have the chance. As the saying goes, "The purpose in life is to find your gifts and give them away." When your best self is activated, you'll light up. You'll feel that you're making the best possible use of your time on this planet.

CHAPTER 4

Changing Your Story Once It's in Motion

"Individuals do not change fundamentally
in who they are without a very serious
personal crisis of some kind."

—SUMANTRA GHOSHAL

G hoshal's quote reflects the reality and power of habit. In life, we sometimes find ourselves in a rut instead of a groove. The rut is a set of behaviors that are so well worn that we can't even remember why we do them. Like a deep channel worn in rock by water, it can be hard to shift in a new direction and make new habits.

If you have ever been in a rut, you know how hard it is to break free. Ghoshal reminds us that sometimes trauma helps us make major changes in our lives. Even though the word "trauma" summons up thoughts of negative life events, some trauma is positive, like graduating from high school or university, or having a baby. We'll see in this chapter that it is not only negative trauma that helps us experience change. We'll explore how creating and immersing yourself in your personal highlight reel can create "positive trauma," and we'll see why that is a good thing when it comes to changing your habits and pursuing more of your potential.

POST-TRAUMATIC GROWTH

I want to tell you a story about Todd Lockwood, a photographer and music producer in Burlington, Vermont. Back in the early 1970s, a friend gave Lockwood a novel by Richard Brautigan as a gift (with the unfortunate title of *The Abortion*). The friend had written a little inscription inside that said, "This book will change your life."

Turns out, this inscription was correct.

The novel describes a library where regular people can come and drop off their own unpublished books. No book is turned away, and the books get to live there forever. Of course, the novel was surreal. How could anything like this library exist in real life? Lockwood became fascinated by the novel and the idea of the library. Some might say obsessed. He ended up reading the book about once a year for the next fifteen years.

Lockwood said, "Every time I'd read it, I'd get the same feeling from it. First thing I would say to myself is, 'When is somebody going to build this library?' To eventually becoming, 'When am *I* going to?'"

Lockwood kept delaying his dream, but throughout his life he continued thinking, "I'll put that library together someday." And then one day Lockwood's sister died, when a United DC-10 flight crashed in Sioux City, Iowa. According to Lockwood, "Losing a sibling is one of those things that really causes you to look at the things that you've done in your life and ask yourself, are these really the best things I can be doing right now?"

This was almost the same sentiment expressed by Rebecca, who you met in the introduction, after her grandmother died. Rebecca's response was to boycott the classes that fixated on her deficiencies and instead focus on the areas in her life she enjoyed and exceled in, such as theater. When Lockwood's sister died, his response was to start his library for unpublished books, as described in *The Abortion*.

Lockwood remembers he was watching the movie *Field of Dreams*. He said, "About halfway into that film, it became really obvious to me that Brautigan's library is my baseball field. If I build it, people will come." He felt like this library was what he was made to do.

Lockwood opened his library in Burlington in a little building next to the Institute of Massage Therapy. Lockwood's library was home for anyone with a burning need to express anything. There seemed to be a desire for it, because shortly after opening people started bringing in books they had written. There's a science fiction novel called *It's the Queen of Darkness, Pal*, written by an anonymous sewer worker. Another person brought in *Leather Clothes and the History of Man*, which is somehow made entirely of leather, pages and all.

Richard Brautigan, the author of *The Abortion*, came into the library himself with a book called *Moose*. One book is called *Bacon Death*, a greasy book that actually looks like a pound of bacon. The library's most prolific contributor is Albert E. Helzner, who has contributed nineteen books (three under a pseudonym!).

Lockwood's "Very Public Library" isn't something he created for wealth or fame. He just felt a strong, persistent need over fifteen years to express himself through this library. After he lost his sister, it became his labor of love and a defining feature of his life (he's had to move the library three times). As he says, "The beauty of it is that it doesn't make sense."

Turns out, other people also see the beauty of it. Lockwood's unique form of self-expression has been covered by BBC Radio, the *New York Times*, and the *Wall Street Journal*. Hundreds of papers across the United States covered the story. An arts festival in Seattle asked Lockwood to set up a mini version of the library at the festival. And you can listen to a show about it on *This American Life*.

The point of me telling you Lockwood's story in *this* book is to show you how trauma can sometimes help us become exceptional. Lockwood nursed a persistent desire to contribute something unique to the world for a decade and a half. The library was something that he felt he needed to do. But for many years he stuck to the script of his life, going through the motions, living at his own average. Which, by the way, was an extremely good average! He had a great life and a great job, but his sister's plane crash reminded him that death is not only mandatory, but it can also come surprisingly soon.

Life is transient. It's powerful to remember that we may not have much time to pursue our dreams, express our unique perspectives, and contribute something of meaning to the world.

Negative personal events, like serious illness or losing a family member or friend, can sometimes lead to positive personal transformation. It may sound like a Zen principle, but it is an empirical phenomenon. A growing body of science in clinical psychology and personality research calls this *post-traumatic growth*. This research stream was reviewed by Eranda Jayawickreme, professor of psychology at Wake Forest University, and Laura Blackie, University of Nottingham. Their book starts with the assumption that post-traumatic growth is actually a form of positive personality change. In their review of the research literature, they found that between 58% and 83% of participants report growth after trauma.

For example, a grieving father who experienced the tragedy of losing his son to a drunk driver might become aware that the life of every one of us is finite. He might realize that he was taking his relationships for granted, when really he should be savoring them as a gift. As a result of his son's death, he might prioritize these relationships higher in his life, invest deeper into them, and find greater fulfillment in them.

It might sound a little counterintuitive, but this is how shock can help us transform the paths we are on. Sometimes it takes a jolt in life to help us appreciate its brevity, make a change, and motivate us to live up to our full potential.

A BONUS ROUND IN LIFE

Lots of us have our own version of a life jolt that helped us grow and pursue more living out of life. If we make it through the difficult times—the crucible—we sometimes look back on it as the anvil of adversity upon which our character was forged.

In his memoir *No Such Thing as a Bad Day*, the American politician Hamilton Jordan described how his battle with cancer changed him:

> *After my first cancer, even the smallest joys in life took on a special meaning—watching a beautiful sunset, a hug from my child, a laugh with [my wife] Dorothy. That feeling has not diminished with time. After my second and third cancers, the simple joys of life are everywhere and are boundless, as I cherish my family and friends and contemplate the rest of my life, a life I certainly do not take for granted.*

In the introduction, I began telling you about my own cancer story. I want to return to that story here, because, in the end, like Jordan, I experienced deep growth from it. It helped my partner Alison and I question some assumptions about how much time we have on this earth and what we really want to be doing with that time.

When I got my diagnosis, Alison and I had been living in North Carolina for over ten years. Five years after we arrived, I felt I'd already learned most of what I was going to learn there. Personally, I knew it stifled me to live in a little university town in the southern United States, and it felt like I was going through the motions. For years, I had known that it was not a good fit for me, but rather than seek out our next adventure in life, it just seemed easier to stay the course in North Carolina for another year. And then another.

What I really wanted to do was go live in another country. When I was twenty years old, I lived with a family in Todi, Italy, as part of a university exchange. Fast-forward fifteen years, Alison and I loved the thrill of experiencing new cultures together. Each year we would take one ten-day vacation—Spain, or Italy, the Netherlands, that sort of thing. We would come back to North Carolina feeling full throttle with energy and life, but returning to my real life made me feel a deep sadness. I could feel my soul ache.

That ache would last for weeks. My reaction was always, "Well, that's what it means to become an adult."

And so I would struggle to settle back into a routine I was bored with. Of course, even if I acknowledged to myself that I yearned to move, it just didn't seem realistic to leave the United States. It was simpler and more efficient to just stay put. There were too many details with life to change, when everything was so settled. Our kids went to a good school, house payments were in place. The cars needed to be inspected, the oil changed. You know the drill.

I had known for years that I was uninspired with my own life, with myself. But I pushed that thought to the back of my mind. After all, there would always be time to re-engage with life later on.

Same thing with my work. I had let myself down there too in the name of efficiency, by making myself into a robot. I had a set of slides I used each time I taught. I had created them in a previous decade. I said the same words the same way so many times that I would often "shut off" and watch myself give the performance from the ceiling. The same jokes worked in the same places. I can remember other professors nudging me to try teaching something new, because they could see I was half shut off. And maybe they had been there before in their own lives. But my class evaluations were favorable, so I didn't see the point in reinventing the class. It was just more efficient to teach the class as I had always done one more year. And then another.

You know that "possibility thinking" that many of us experience when we are young and planning our lives and careers—anything is possible! Well, that had turned into "probability thinking" for me— that is, living life by following the path of least resistance.

I accepted the tediousness of life as part of growing up. Since I had a good job and was making lots of money, it felt like I just needed to trudge through it all on the way to retirement. I remember one day I was telling a good friend my goal was to buy and rent ten houses in the little college town, so then I could retire (we already had three). My wise friend looked at me hard and said, "Dan, something is wrong with you. You're not supposed to be thinking about retirement at thirty-five." I pretended to myself that she didn't know what she was talking about. Somehow that was more comforting than admitting that she did.

A similar dynamic had taken control of my relationship with my partner, Alison. We had been together since we were in college. We were good roommates, but for years we were not communicating about important issues. We were really struggling with intimacy. I pushed all those issues to the back of my mind for a long time, because having difficult conversations is, well, difficult. Looking back now, I guess it felt too scary to be honest and rock that boat. So I accepted this too was part of what happened when you were married a long time. Part of growing up.

Essentially, I capitulated on my own life.

All this changed for me when my cancer trauma forced me to stop ignoring my transience. Once I was jolted into seeing some of the assumptions I had adopted about life, I could see many of them were not working anymore. I saw that I had been living—maybe for five or six years—as if the goal of life was a safe, efficient trip to the grave. I couldn't remember what particular day, or what year, I let that belief take hold, but once I was shaken into seeing it, I could fight back against it.

After coming to terms with my transience, I saw that I didn't have forever to get around to "being me." Of course, I already *knew* I didn't have forever, but I was not *acting* as though I believed it. With my assumptions shaken by trauma, I saw that it was wrong for me to sleepwalk my way through life. Even though the life and habits I had created were successful and lucrative, I could now see that did not mean that I was chained to them.

My trauma also allowed me to see that "just get through it until retirement" was not an acceptable answer to my life dissatisfaction. As the godfather of modern mindfulness, Jon Kabat-Zinn, once said, "When it comes right down to it, the challenge of mindfulness is to realize that 'this is it. Right now is my life. And I accept that.'"

Trauma shatters our basic schemas, which we then must rebuild and modify. Survivors of trauma are worse off in many ways, but other changes can be positive. We can gain wisdom, insight, and empathy.

For my part, I was lucky and I got a reprieve. One crisp summer morning I was riding my bicycle to work about three months into my chemo treatments. Most of the cancer had already melted away, and as I looked around I felt a joyful wave crest over me, and I suddenly heard myself say out loud, "I just might make it!" I felt a swell of hope that made my eyes tear up. I had received a delicious new sense, a fantastic new way of seeing. And what I could see was that my life was an adventure that I had the fortunate chance to experience. It was not a chore I had to get through.

This jolt motivated me to improve my engagement with my life. Alison and I started down the long, difficult road of open communication by talking to a counselor to improve our relationship. Saying what you actually *mean* takes courage after many years of avoiding disagreements and not saying what you mean. Coming close to death helped me see that Alison and I didn't have forever to improve our relationship.

I also recognized that the things I thought I possessed—like houses and cars and furniture and a well-paying job—had started to possess me. These things, over the years, had somehow become my problems instead of my solutions. They were holding me back from becoming my version of exceptional.

So, we reprioritized. We found that we could refocus all the particular details of our lives—like our cars and house and kids' schools—so that they were the background of life instead of what directed us. We moved to London, first for three months, and then a year, and then indefinitely. What had seemed almost impossible to change felt pretty easy to do with this new mindset—sell the cars, rent the house, and pursue what was most important to us while we still could.

Moving to a new country and experiencing a new culture was an incredible shift. But moving was not going to fix everything if

I continued to act the same way. So I started changing my habits at work too. I started researching and teaching new topics, pursuing ideas I had been interested in for years but just hadn't been sure if I could successfully pull off. I started showing up in my teaching—actually speaking with students and executives in real time, instead of working off of decade-old scripted presentations. It took courage not knowing where the conversation in the classroom would go, but it meant I was present and excited to be teaching again.

This jolt resulted in a strong feeling of getting a "bonus round" in life. In a way, it feels like being a ghost. Kind of like I already died, but somehow I got a second lifetime to appreciate being alive. All these days since I finished chemo I got for free. Perhaps this is what "Coma Dave" felt too. Even if I died today, I already got an extra decade to watch my kids grow into people I admire and respect. Whatever time and experiences I get now feel like "extra" life.

Of course, you also have that same bonus time. Just as I myself had bonus time for the ten years *before* I got cancer. It just didn't seem that way. It can be hard to see time as a gift when we ignore transience and when we feel *entitled* to good health and life. Like Dave in chapter 2, I learned that life is fragile, and trauma can sometimes lead to incredible, life-changing paths.

★ *Wake Up to Life* ★

Take fifteen minutes and write about what you would change in your life if you got a "bonus round."

Here are a few questions to get you started.

- What do you love working on that you would shift your time and attention toward doing even more?

- What would make you feel more alive, vibrant, enthusiastic, and excited about your life?

- Are there any ways that you are disappointed in yourself? How long do you plan to allow that disappointment to persist?

- What would you regret most if you knew you only had six more months to live? What have you allowed to move you from "possibility thinking" into "probability thinking"?

- What can you reprioritize so that you are pursuing your life goals and dreams? What's holding you back from going after it?

When you are finished with the exercise, add this in your highlight reel folder.

Return to this exercise any time you feel stuck or find yourself in one of life's ruts. Reflecting on these questions can be a powerful reminder to make the most of our lives and appreciate the time we've been given.

POSITIVE TRAUMA

In the most recent—and arguably best—meta-analysis of post-traumatic growth, psychologist Judith Mangelsdorf and her colleagues claim that "there is a strong negativity bias" in the research studies. They report that only about 25% of post-traumatic growth studies focus on positive events.

At this point, you might be asking yourself, "Wait a minute, can trauma *be* positive? Is that even a *thing*?!"

That's because we usually associate "trauma" with negative life events, like a serious illness, death, or emotional pain. We sometimes forget that life also can offer us positive trauma. Like falling in love. If you don't remember how traumatic falling in love is, you probably haven't done it for a while. Positive trauma also can emerge when you get a big promotion or a great new job. These are highly positive events for most people, but they also come with a huge disruption to our lives.

The research shows that people grow from both positive and negative trauma. The growth reveals itself in terms of improved self-esteem, deeper relationships, more meaning in life, and enhanced spirituality.

We all know Friedrich Nietzsche's quote "That which does not kill us makes us stronger." But sometimes it also is true that what makes you much happier also can make you stronger. In fact, the empirical research suggests that positive trauma is just as effective for personal growth as negative trauma. Although some researchers argue that negative life events should have a stronger impact on our lives, Mangelsdorf's meta-analysis rejects that claim: "We found no general evidence for the widespread conviction that negative life events have a stronger effect than positive ones."

This is where the power of your highlight reel comes in.

As part of creating your personal highlight reel, people who know you well are going to write their memories about the positive impact you make on their lives. Similar to Dave in chapter 2, your personal highlight reel can trigger post-traumatic growth, and you will likely receive a positive jolt from the experience of reading these memories.

When we hear personal, gritty stories about our contributions from people we trust, we often experience positive trauma. Laura Morgan Roberts and her colleagues called it an *appreciation jolt*— an extraordinarily good but surprising event that creates strong emotions. Research suggests that you might feel a jolt of pride and positive emotions as the people you love crystalize and validate the best version of you through their stories. As we'll see later, you will likely feel gratitude and humility that people took time to write meaningful and appreciative stories about you.

People can grow in important ways in the face of hardship, no question about that. However, as Gretchen Spreitzer, professor of management at the University of Michigan and expert on best-self activation, explained, we often react to threats with paralysis and inflexibility. Whereas positive trauma, like an *appreciation jolt,* can result in a more expansive kind of personal growth:

> *In the face of adversity, threat rigidity research finds that individuals close down and regress to past learned behaviors, rather than seeking out learning and growth. Unlike threatening challenges that imply real potential for failure or harm, positive jolts imply the possibility of gains, and thus energize individuals.*

Positive jolts emerged in many of my interviews with people who had constructed their personal highlight reels. I wish I could share them all with you, because they really are fascinating, but here are just a few examples of what I mean.

I met fifty-nine-year-old José Luis while he was visiting from Mexico City to attend a two-week executive program at London Business School. José read his personal highlight reel for the first time right before he went for a run in Regent's Park. He runs every week, but he told me that during this run, he had an epiphany. While jogging and thinking through all the stories he had read in his highlight reel, suddenly he noticed "everybody else moving in slow motion" as his own running quickened and felt more and more effortless.

José told me that it was "the strangest sensation in my life. I didn't know how to describe it, actually, when I came back home. I only talk about this with my wife because I thought 'everybody's going to think that I'm crazy.'" Of course, neither José Luis nor I know what was happening chemically in his brain—what beautiful concoction of dopamine and serotonin and endorphins were mixed together. But it would seem that by reflecting on the sum of his highlight reel José had a sudden jolt of energy, something resembling a runner's high. And the result of this experience was palpable and powerful. José said it helped him take a big step back from his "normal life and habits" and begin to think about how he might do more with his strengths to improve his life.

Another example of an appreciation jolt comes from forty-eight-year-old Louise, a high-powered partner in a global consulting firm in Chicago and someone who demands a high degree of professionalism from herself and others. It is not easy to earn partnership as a woman in a masculine business environment, and Louise is not often prone to sentimentality. However, after reading her highlight reel, Louise told me how it had a strong emotional effect on her:

> *I think I was more emotional than happy. Happy is not the right word. Touched. Yes, really touched. Moved. Like it was almost romantic. I have to say, none of what they wrote I was not aware of. I think, rationally, I kind of knew everything they wrote. But the fact that they tell you with their own words, what they've seen, and how great you are, is very touching.*

Louise was affected in several ways by this appreciation jolt, but perhaps the key change she made was not getting "super angry at people" for their errors, such as a mistake in a presentation. She used to become irate, and even yell at people, but now she says she has adjusted her style to try to give the necessary feedback but not be "so stubborn about it." Louise told me that once she understood how much more powerful focusing on the positive could be, she began building on people's strengths rather than targeting their mistakes and flaws.

Remember Ron, the young journalism student at the University of Michigan whose girlfriend convinced him to create his highlight reel after he experienced doubts? Ron described his positive trauma like this:

> *I was so shocked when I read these stories. This exercise has really challenged my beliefs about myself because it is*

real tangible evidence that disproves many of the negative thoughts I have about myself. This has proved to me that I have some really wonderful strengths and that I can be a valuable contribution.

Throughout the interviews I conducted, what I heard again and again, across diverse age groups and national cultures, was a sense of positive trauma. People regularly use words like "intensity," "surprised," "amazed," "stunned," "touched," and "wonder."

Even when trauma is positive, it may not feel entirely comfortable to you as you read your own highlight reel. For example, when I spoke with forty-three-year-old Emma, a consulting firm partner in Charlotte, North Carolina, she told me, "It was hard not to read through that and just have an overwhelming sense of love and appreciation . . . A little bit like, 'Oh, stop, I can't hear. Too much good about myself.'"

My partner Alison experienced a similar discomfort when she read her highlight reel for the first time. In fact, after Alison read one or two of the stories, she put her highlight reel away and didn't take it out again for weeks. When she eventually pulled it back out and read some more, she felt really reluctant to read about herself at her best—almost as if it were immoral. We have learned to call this resistance "modesty."

If you stop to think about it, Emma's and Alison's reactions to their highlight reels are really interesting. And I think a bit counterintuitive. These reactions are almost the opposite of what many people predict, which is "you'll make people arrogant if you tell them only positive feedback."

Yet, Emma's and Alison's reactions are not altogether rare. This comes up for a few people almost every single time I debrief a highlight reel session. Many say they feel a little reluctant to "turn the page," and they experience a shiver of anxiety as they are about to read their next highlight, even though they know people only wrote about their positive impact.

This is the eulogy delay at work, creating this seemingly natural discomfort as we read about our strengths and who we are at our best. It's what holds us back from sharing our appreciation for each other and getting closer to one another.

The point is this: Like Dave reading his own eulogies on social media, this series of stories from loved ones can disrupt our assumptions and offer us a different narrative about our possible selves. One person told me after reading his highlight reel that the experience was "unimaginably powerful. It has transformed my perspective and broken the shackles of the past." Of course, different people respond in different ways. But for many, a personal highlight reel can surprise and jolt you into seeing the impact you are capable of making.

Many of us are our own worst critics as we go through life. Our negative assumptions and negative self-talk can make life seem like a daily struggle. It can lead to downward spirals or keep us in ruts that hold us back from our potential. A highlight reel can jolt you into a more positive cycle and create real personal change.

Ordinarily you would never get to hear these remarkable stories about yourself, because too often people wait until the end. In step 2 you will get to do just that. Your highlight reel will give you a glimpse into how others perceive you when you are at your best and lead you to ask yourself the important questions about the path you're on. When you discover your strengths and find out how to tap into them, it has a way of waking you up to the life you were meant to be living.

STEP 2

CHAPTER 5

Put Your Best Dress in the Window

I n the first step you learned the science behind the positive method and how it can transform your habits. We saw how improving your narrative can change your reality. By focusing on your strengths you can move beyond your own average, activating your best possible self.

Now in step 2, you will create your personal highlight reel using the positive method. You'll begin by *reflecting* on some of your own specific memories of times when you have been exceptional. Then, you'll write to people in your social network, sharing your *gratitude* and memories about times they have been exceptional. Finally, you'll *gather evidence* of times you were at your best by asking people in your social network to share their memories.

Your personal highlight reel will serve as a powerful self-affirmation. Some of the best research in psychology suggests this self-affirmation allows us to access the full potential of our brains. It does this by helping us overcome the wasteful mental nagging of self-doubt and the downward spiral of negative self-talk.

So far, so good, right? Who wouldn't want to try an evidenced-based way of becoming your best self? Well . . . I've got to tell you, the positive method does not always come easily to everyone. The force of the eulogy delay makes many people feel awkward about creating their highlight reel. Over the years, I've become convinced that our allergic reaction to focusing on strengths is due to a cultural apprehension about pride, and that this is the driving force behind the eulogy delay. Once you understand how you can move effectively around this force, you can get to work on the positive method.

PRIDE: VICE AND VIRTUE

Pride is one of the seven deadly sins. In fact, lots of smart people think it's the worst of the seven. Theologian Thomas Aquinas said, "Inordinate self-love is the cause of every sin." Philosophers criticize pride as a sort of gateway sin because they believe it opens the door to let the other sins enter. Don't tell money, but according to this logic, pride is actually the root of all evil.

Our modern relationship with pride clearly is a bit more complex. For example, if you were to look up pride in the Oxford dictionary, it would first be defined as "a feeling of deep pleasure or satisfaction derived from one's own achievements." That doesn't sound *so* terrible, does it?

Here's the second definition: "Confidence and self-respect as expressed by members of a group." Again, that doesn't sound too bad. Did I miss a memo? Is it just me, or do "confidence" and "self-respect" strike you as good things?

And the third definition: "Consciousness of one's own dignity." Hmm, that is not giving me a root-of-all-evil kind of vibe. In fact, I think that I might want my own children to be conscious of their own dignity!

It is not until we get to a subcategory of this third definition that we see "having an excessively high opinion of oneself or one's importance." Bingo! *This* is the source of the old-school and Old Testament social norms against pride.

Traditionally, pride has been paired up with self-absorption, conceit, vanity, and egotism. This type of arrogant pride is not good for community, and humans are very communal creatures. Throughout evolution, our ancestors found it very hard to survive on their own. We humans just don't have many physiological advantages over other animals. We don't have big sharp teeth or claws for attacking. We don't have shells on our backs for defense. We aren't very strong compared to gorillas and apes. Ten thousand years ago, if you were ostracized and pushed outside your community, you could not survive for long.

We humans have a lengthy history of survival-through-community, and community requires people to work together.

When people have arrogant pride, they think they are better than others, or are too good to help out with necessary group work. You can see how this might cause problems or conflict within a community. If someone believes themselves to be better than everyone else, they can also become complacent and unmotivated when it comes to self-improvement or working for the greater good. Arrogant, complacent people also typically do not have a quick-to-learn mentality and can be self-focused. This makes it extremely difficult to trust that these individuals are acting for the good of the whole or contributing fairly to a team.

Let's face it: At their worst, people with arrogant pride can be self-serving terrors. They destroy community and slash at the social fabric.

So, across time, society has developed strong social norms to punish pride. Parents are expected to punish conceit in their children. Groups and teams punish arrogance and vanity in team members through criticism, ridicule, and ostracism. Religion plays its part in punishing pride: People guilty of committing the sin of pride are "broken on the wheel" for eternity in hell (who even thinks these punishments up?). Greek myths taught that we will be struck down by the gods for pride, as Icarus was when his vanity led him to fly too close to the sun and his wings melted; he died and his father Daedalus lost a child.

Put this all together, and we see that traditional society has been sending us a consistent message: that we should be *modest*. We should ridicule people who highlight their unique worth. We should focus on our weaknesses, not on our strengths.

And I believe we understand implicitly how our culture asks us to choose modesty over pride. Remember Tracey, the actress and economics major at the University of Michigan? After reading her highlight reel, she recognized how hard it was to shake that guilt we feel when openly acknowledging our strengths:

> *It's an incredible opportunity to see what others think of you, and how that compares to how you see yourself. It's hard in the first place to focus on the positive aspects of one's self, but our society makes it harder by shaming pride.*

Our long-standing societal anxiety about arrogant pride results in the eulogy delay. We only get comfortable focusing on people's strengths when they are not around anymore to get a big head about it. And this is why you might feel awkward completing some of step 2. Even though the science supports it, you might find that traditional social norms make it feel uncomfortable to focus on what you do best. Some people even feel a need to ridicule this process.

Many of us fear that if we focus on the positive, other people—or we ourselves—might become vain and smug. In my structured interviews, more than half of the people I spoke with, from Seoul to Sydney to New Jersey, spontaneously mentioned the cultural resistance to focusing on strengths. As we will see, this fear is misplaced when it comes to highlight reels. In fact, the opposite is true. People feel inspired and energized to use their strengths even more, and give more to others, after reading their highlights.

I want to introduce Rhee, who we will come back to several times over the course of this book. In terms of background, Rhee was raised in a tiny house in Seoul, Korea. He and his brother and sister rarely saw their father, who had become a CEO at the young age of thirty-eight and almost always came home from work very late, after they were asleep. Growing up, Rhee's parents never said they were proud of him because it was not part of their culture.

Twenty-eight years later, Rhee is working in Singapore as a partner at Boston Consulting Group, focusing on financial institutions across Southeast Asia. As part of an executive education program I was running, Rhee created his highlight reel.

Rhee told me that the highlight reel seemed completely countercultural to him. He was used to receiving critical feedback, from his father, his teachers, and his work colleagues. But never in his life had people only focused on positive feedback. When he asked his wife to write her memories of him at his best, she actually laughed. "I don't know what to write about you," she told him. "I can write bad things about you all night long, but writing something good about you, that would be a very difficult task."

Rhee found it even more difficult asking his work colleagues. As he said, it is just not done in schools or at work, because the focus is always on addressing limitations: "We are conditioned to find out 'what are the problems?' We're so good at finding the negative." Even in families this resistance prevails. Rhee told me, "We never say, 'Hey, son. I'm so proud of you because of this.' You never do it that way. It seems like a joke."

Clearly, Rhee felt the heavy force of the eulogy delay, but he pushed right back, and in the end received stories and memories from twelve different people, including his wife. She described how when she wanted to return to school, or whenever she asked Rhee to do something, he put her request above all the other things in his life. She explained how valuable it made her feel when "you put my needs on full priority, and you really take care of things."

The highlight reel experience was powerful for Rhee. He said, "It's far deeper than I ever imagined." It helped him improve the way he connects with other people. Now, Rhee regularly focuses on people's positive contributions when he talks with his team about their performance. Rhee told me he gets far greater results from the same people when he asks them to do more of what they are best at. In his words:

We have been completely wrong in how we manage people.
You can save energy by leveraging the muscle that already

exists. There is more power in our strengths. The world can be much, much better this way.

Rhee's experience was certainly not isolated. In interview after interview, I learned how many people had to reimagine their relationship with pride in order to reach out to their network, and then to accept the positive affirmations revealed in those stories. After they read their highlight reels, they felt motivated to contribute more at work and in their relationships, and they felt more connected to their community.

On the other side of the world, I found a very similar resistance to the highlight reel when I interviewed forty-six-year-old Brian from Chatham, New Jersey, about reaching out for his stories. He said he found it really surprising how normal it is for us to make a phone call to a family member, or find an hour to chat with an old friend. That doesn't seems like a big deal, but he said it feels like a way bigger hurdle asking someone to sit down and write their best memories of you—not because of the time commitment, but because it is so rare to ask for complimentary feedback in American culture. After reading his report, Brian said, "You know that there's a lot of love. And positive emotion, and admiration, and all of that. Which everyone wants more of in their life! But somehow asking for that is awkward."

If you had never thought about the force of the eulogy delay, you might struggle to understand the source of Brian's discomfort. It's not just people's time you are asking for; it is asking them to focus their attention on your best characteristics that creates the discomfort. Unless we confront this issue with pride, it will continue to hold us back and push us away from reflecting on what we appreciate most about each other.

TAKING PRIDE IN YOUR GIFTS

Louise, the hardworking partner in the Chicago consulting firm who we met in the last chapter, said she recognized that the stigma against positive feedback starts with the school system, which "is very much about the things you do wrong and not the things you do right."

She pointed out how we spend so much time being marked down and held back by our mistakes, and how this focus then transitions from school into work, where "you focus on the flaws of people because you're trying to get them to correct what they don't do well. You don't think about building on the things they do well."

Louise found the focus on her strengths in the highlight reel to be very motivating, and it has helped her as a leader in her firm. She used to worry a lot about speaking in front of groups, for example. Even though it was part of her role to give speeches, it unnerved her. But her general ability as a good communicator emerged as one of the strong and consistent themes in her stories across family, friends, and colleagues. This encouraged her to take pride in her public speaking and to do more of it. She began to see speeches as interpersonal communication instead of an "event." As Louise put it, "Seeing that consistency in my report is helping me today when I have to do these things. I'm feeling more confidence."

When we allow ourselves to feel a healthy dose of pride in our strengths, we are leaning into those qualities and owning them with confidence and grace. We are not letting our gifts lie dormant.

Just like Olympic athletes become more motivated after watching their highlight reels, across countless interviews and highlight reel studies I also found that people worked harder, are more creative, made customers happier, and made fewer mistakes when they experience a grounded sense of pride in their capabilities and strengths.

Barbara Fredrickson, a psychology professor and one of the parents of the positive psychology field, describes pride not as a problem, but as a solution. She defines pride as the emotion we feel when we see our positive impact on the world and on other people. It's that sweet boost to our self-esteem for a job well done. When pride is viewed this way, it helps explain why highlight reels do not make us arrogant and complacent.

Instead, pride is motivational, because it creates the urge to imagine and pursue even bigger accomplishments. This is why pride can help us build those upward spirals of self-improvement that we have seen again and again in the research.

We all have times when we reach our own version of exceptional. We all have personal strengths that allow us to make unique contributions to our families, to our schools, to our teams, and to our communities.

Too much humility can *waste* our strengths. According to Michael Eric Dyson, professor of religious and Africana studies at UPenn, "If you are trying to pretend through false humility that you are not as great as you're supposed to be . . . then you're committing a sin as well, because you're refusing to live up to the greatness that is inherent in you."

The next section of this chapter will help you reflect on and write your own stories for your highlight reel. This might be a new activity for you, which means it may feel a little strange because you have not practiced it. Remember, social convention trains us to call this awkwardness "modesty."

But get this: If we are not careful, our resistance to recognizing our best self comes with a real cost. Research shows that when it feels difficult to bring stories to mind, your mind can interpret this difficulty as *evidence* that the stories are not true. This is called "meta cognition"—when your mind is aware of your thinking patterns and is keeping track of how hard it is to develop your stories about yourself. So if it seems awkward to recall and write stories about your best self, your brain might try to infer that your peak memories are not your "true" self.

Crazy human brains.

This discomfort is normal, and exactly what we are going to break down, through practice, across the course of this book. The more you bring forward these positive stories about yourself, the stronger you make the linkages, and the more your mind accepts them as truth as they begin to feel ingrained. This is positive self-affirmation.

So just work through the forthcoming steps, and remember that it takes time to make new behaviors feel natural. In life, everything that seems easy now—like writing or walking—felt difficult at first. We need to normalize the difficulty that comes when we practice behavioral change, because you can't transform your life without getting comfortable with the uncomfortable.

IT'S TIME TO PUT YOUR BEST DRESS IN THE WINDOW

If you ran a clothing store, what would you put in the window? Something from last year that didn't sell very well? Or would you place your best dress in the window? Something that you think represents your store at its best?

The following exercise will help you identify what makes you extraordinary, so you can put this in the window. It's time to bring those memories of who you are at your best to the front of your mind.

Dan McAdams, professor of psychology at Northwestern University, has developed a "life story approach" to identity your stories. McAdams says that the stories we tell about our life experiences are the building blocks of how we define ourselves. This means that when we write about our specific life experiences, we make the stories into something we *are*, not just something that has *happened* to us. Writing about our experiences is a process of self-construction.

By writing about your life experiences, you literally are authoring yourself.

Let's try this together right now. The first step is to block off twenty minutes to just brainstorm. Let your mind wander as you look for specific times in your life where you felt that you were doing what you do best.

Dredge your memories for five or six specific times that you felt you were using your character traits, skills, and interests to make your best contributions. Think through different contexts in your life: home, vacation, work, friendships, family, relationships, and more. It might be helpful to think about times when it felt that you were "doing what you were made to do." It might also be helpful to think about events where time seemed to go away because you were so immersed in an activity that you "lost yourself" in flow. Maybe some of your best-self memories were from the last few years, while others happened a long time ago.

As you are brainstorming, jot down a few notes and ideas. Don't try to write up whole stories just yet. First, just list a bunch of possibilities to choose from.

Then, after you have a good list of five or six possibilities, pick at least three of these instances to write about. For each of these three memories, spend about fifteen to twenty minutes writing out the event in detail.

Remember, you're going to get out of this what you put into it. You have seen that there is solid science showing the power in self-affirmation and in best-self activation. But for this to work you need to move far away from generalities, such as "I am lovable" or "I am intelligent." You need to remember and write about the key peculiarities of the situation that made your particular heart sing.

And the research suggests that just *thinking* about these events is not enough—it is writing about them that helps your brain process them and internalize them. If you're just reading this book and skipping the exercises, it's like reading about doing pull-ups. Reading won't make your biceps stronger.

Here is some advice as you write about each of your memories.

- **Write up each of these events as a *story*, not just a collection of facts.** Make your story have a beginning, a middle, and an end. Our brains are literally built for stories, which is why we remember stories so much better than facts. Research on this type of expressive writing shows that writing about your best self will make you happier and healthier by increasing clarity about your values and priorities, resulting in a coherent narrative about yourself.

- **As you write about each event, try to relive the moment in your mind.** Locate the specific details as you write. Replay the memory in your mind, and write about any gritty, distinct elements of the event that you remember. Research by Joanne Wood and her team at the University of Waterloo showed that repeating trite self-building maxims (for example, "I am confident and bold") actually *reduced* the self-esteem of people with low self-esteem when the statement didn't align with their actions and real feelings.

  In life, we don't want to simply be praised—we want to act in ways that are *praiseworthy*. When self-affirmations lack credibility and are not attached to personal behaviors and specific events, they can backfire among those of us who could most use them. This is why we want to write out our stories with great detail so we can ground our strengths with tangible evidence.

- **Make sure you answer these questions about each event:** Where were you? Who was with you or around you? What were you doing and how were you behaving? What was the result of your actions? Who was affected, and how were they affected? How did you feel at that moment? Try to relive the feelings, and then write about them.

When you are finished with the exercise, add it to your highlight reel folder.

By making the stories in your highlight reel specific and behavioral, you are strengthening the mental connection between yourself, your peak behaviors, and the good emotions surrounding them. This exercise is the first step to making your best self *chronically accessible.* As we learned in chapter 3, the story that is at the forefront of your mind is the one that is activated, or working.

When you intentionally pull forward these positive stories of who you are by writing about them, it makes it more likely you'll act that way in the future.

This also helps you make hard trade-offs in life and better decisions in the future. Like the alcoholics who knew what their best selves would do when they were tempted to drink and were mentally prepared to make healthier choices for themselves. And the low-income students who chose not to disturb their class and spend more time studying, because they had created a new concept of their best selves in an academic setting.

At this point, you have at least three stories full of details about times you have been exceptional. Congratulations! You are on your way. The research suggests that this new identity that you are creating of you at your best is already feeling a little more cohesive and affirmed. These personal memories show you what you are capable of when you reach your potential. Just by focusing on your positive stories, you'll also have more stamina and resilience if you're dealing with any stress or obstacles today that might cause you to question yourself.

But, like Dave in chapter 2, you do not yet have full or accurate information about your best possible self. It is enlightening, and often surprising, to learn what the people who are closest to you perceive as most valuable about you. They know better than you how you affect them, just as you recognize better than they do what is extraordinary about them. Words from others can deliver a powerful transformational jolt. Hearing our own eulogies in the form of a highlight reel can wake us up to our potential.

CHAPTER 6

Create Your Personal Highlight Reel

I n his wonderful book *Lost Connections*, Johann Hari talks about the real causes of depression and anxiety and how to heal ourselves. Hari argues, "It turns out the self isn't the solution. The only answer lies beyond it." Hari proposes that instead of only looking inward to improve our lives, we must reach out and give to others. And, if we want to feel deep fulfillment and happiness with ourselves, we first need to learn from others how we add to their worlds. We need to learn what we can contribute to them that is unique and valuable.

That is why, for your highlight reel, you can't stop with just writing your own narratives and memories about yourself. You need to reach outside, to your community—to the people whose worlds you want to improve, and the people you want to learn from.

There are just two major behaviors that you will practice in this chapter:

1. **Pay it forward.** Select someone you know well and admire or appreciate. Write down a memory or two about a specific time they used their unique strengths to make a positive impact in your life or someone else's. Share these memories

with them, to help them begin their own highlight reel. This will also provide a model for them when they write highlight reel stories for you.

2. **Assemble your highlights.** When you share your gratitude stories with others, tell them you'd love to hear a story from them about yourself. Do they have a memory or two of you at your best? Gather up stories across your social network to make up your highlight reel.

That's it. It's not really that hard. I will arm you with the scientific evidence that reveals how beneficial this practice can be for all those family, friends, significant others, and co-workers involved. When you see how much your network and community deeply appreciate hearing these stories from you, it will motivate you to break through the eulogy delay. Your kind words will touch them and they will feel grateful to you and want to give back. There really is no substitute to feeling this for yourself. This give-and-take process opens a door to better relationships and is the core of your highlight reel.

THE POWER OF GRATITUDE

Gratitude is an *emotion*—it is something we feel, not just something we think about rationally. We feel gratitude when we are thankful about something—when we "count our blessings"—particularly if we realize how lucky we are to have the good things in our lives. Often we find that we are thankful for other people who have helped us and added to our lives when they didn't need to.

As an emotion, gratitude energizes us and creates an urge to give something back or to help someone else.

Did you ever wonder why we *have* this emotion?

Remember how humans are not built, physically, for solo survival? Compared to lots of other animals, we are not very fast, or strong. Show me another animal that is still living with its parents when it is ten years old! We're physically vulnerable animals, but as a species we dominate because we are super-social and we build shared dreams. Well, gratitude is a very useful emotion in a species like ours, because it tightens the bonds between people in a community. Why? Because gratitude creates norms of reciprocity—of helping each other—that are extremely useful in creating trust and strong social bonds.

This is why gratitude exists in the first place—gratitude survives as a human emotion because evolutionarily it helped keep our ancestors alive. Our ancestors who possessed this emotion were more likely to live and pass the tendency to feel this emotion on to their children. Who, eventually, became you and me.

Okay, so that is the *evolutionary function* of gratitude. Over the last century, however, gratitude seemed to be on the wane. My colleague Selin Kesebir at the London Business School conducted a study where she and her team researched the frequency of certain words across time. For data, they looked at the 5.2 million books that have been digitized by Google. They observed a strong drop in the words indicating gratitude to others and recognition of one's blessings. Since 1900, they noted that the appearance of the word "gratitude" had fallen by 55%. Thankfulness was down even more, with a decline of 84%.

Unless you have lived under a rock, you are likely aware that these trends are changing once again. Since the field of positive psychology emerged, there has been a large swell of gratitude research. And the data from that research are clear: when we focus on what we are grateful for, we improve our lives.

Being grateful allows us to savor our positive life experiences, which makes the good things in life bright in our brains. Rather than just taking good things for granted, and feeling entitled to them, gratitude reminds us to feel lucky. And it helps us inhibit negative feelings such as envy, bitterness, and greed.

And the best part is that gratitude is *not* just a personality trait. It's not the case that some people get to feel fortunate to experience it, while others are stuck with feeling envious and bitter. *Any* of us can cultivate an attitude of gratitude. Any of us can switch on this emotion by focusing on it and practicing it (just as any of us could allow ourselves to become entitled and take our blessings for granted). This is how the positive method creates more satisfaction in our lives: It gives us the space to participate in giving gratitude and receiving it.

Consider a study by Robert Emmons and Michael McCullough, two professors of psychology. In a series of studies, they instructed a group of participants to engage in self-guided exercises involving "counting their blessings" either on a weekly basis for ten weeks or on a daily basis for two weeks. They put the other participants into various control groups, who focused their attention on routine life events (in one study), daily hassles (in a second study), and comparing themselves to others (in still another study).

Across all their investigations, the people in the gratitude groups reported more positive feelings than the control groups. They also experienced better physical health, better sleep quality, and felt more connected to other people. They were more likely to help other people with personal problems and offer emotional support. Interestingly, people who expressed more gratitude also were more energized and spent more time exercising.

Let's start practicing some gratitude now. First, I'll help you select some people in your network you are thankful for. You'll reflect on times they used their strengths to improve your world, or someone else's. Then, you'll share these memories with them. You don't need to visit them in person (unless you want to!).

Sounds pretty easy, right? And the research shows that this is a powerful way to enhance your relationships. So, why do we not do this more often?

Some insight into this question comes from management professors Amit Kumar at the University of Texas and Nicholas Epley at the University of Chicago. They conducted studies where they asked people to write a letter expressing gratitude to someone who had touched their life in a meaningful way. In the letter, they explained why they were grateful to this person, what this person did for them, and how it affected their life.

After the letters were sent, Kumar and Epley asked the letter-writers to report how the exercise made them feel, from –5 (much more negative than normal) to 5 (much more positive than normal). They also asked them to report how awkward the exercise was for them, from 0 (not at all awkward) to 10 (extremely awkward).

Next, Kumar and Epley also asked the letter-writers to rate how they thought the *recipients* of the letters would feel on the *same* scales and how surprised they thought recipients would be to learn about the specific reasons for their gratitude.

Finally, Kumar and Epley had the recipients of the letters rate how they actually felt upon receiving the letters.

What do you think the results showed? First, as you probably expected, the data confirmed past studies showing that writing a gratitude letter makes people feel more positive. In fact, the letter-writers jumped up more than two points on the positivity scale, compared to how they themselves felt before the process started. So, here we have yet more proof that it feels good to tell others why we appreciate them. It's a real shame we don't do that more often, given that it is free!

But the data also cast direct light on the eulogy delay. Across five independent replications of this same study, results showed that letter-writers substantially *underestimated* how positive recipients would feel reading their gratitude letters. And letter-writers thought that recipients would feel *twice* as awkward as they actually felt.

Results also showed that letter-writers underestimated how surprised recipients would be—both in terms of receiving the gratitude letter and by the content in the letter. Recipients got a much larger positivity jolt than letter-writers predicted.

Here is another misperception: Many letter-writers were concerned that they would not do a good job writing the letters. In reality, the receivers rated them as high as possible in terms of being articulate—well over a nine on a ten-point scale.

This is how a powerful, unseen force can hold us back from expressing gratitude to others. Sadly, this hidden force shuts down an important way to improve our social relationships and well-being.

For example, twenty-year-old Tina was born in Korea and grew up in the Midwest United States in a family that does not express emotions to each other very often. Even though Tina had a good relationship with her sister, they had never spoken to each other about what they valued in their relationship. Tina spoke about these types of things even less with her father and mother.

But after reading her highlight reel, which also included memories from her sister and father, Tina said, "I felt so happy, thankful, and grateful while reading this report. I have realized how amazing the group of people I have around myself is, and how grateful they are to have me as a friend, a daughter, a sister, or a girlfriend." She felt much closer to her family after this process and was motivated to express her appreciation of them more often.

You're not going to fall for the eulogy delay. No way. Because you are armed with data. Equipped with science, you are going to send the gift of gratitude to some people who mean a lot to you. You're going to deepen your relationships. You're going to become exceptional, by being the type of person who catches others doing something right and tells them about it.

For this portion of the positive method, you are going to aim to write gratitude letters to fifteen people. But don't worry—you won't do them all at once! In fact, you'll feel more positive emotions if you spread your writing out across two weeks. Maybe you can focus on writing one letter a day—whatever fits best in your schedule. Once you get started, you may find you want to write more than one story for some people.

You'll probably find that writing for certain people is more enjoyable than writing for others. Some of the people you write for might take more effort. That's okay—it is still valuable. You are just strengthening different relationships from different starting points.

WHO SHOULD I INCLUDE?

Think of fifteen people who are an important part of your life. Some should be friends, some family, some mentors, some significant others, and some colleagues. They may not necessarily be people that you see the most, but, as a group, they know you well across different contexts. Remember, this will eventually be the group of people you ask to share positive memories of you for your highlight reel.

Your list might include a high school friend who you've stayed in touch with over the years and some more recent friends you have gotten to know well over the last year or two. Your group might include a university professor who influenced your career path, a college roommate, and a nurse or doctor you stayed in touch with. For many people, this would include a few people you have worked with, including current or previous colleagues and supervisors. Anyone who knows you well and who you'd like to strengthen your relationship with even more is fair game. The goal is to find a good mix of people you would like to thank and learn from.

Even if it feels awkward at first, or seems strange to include certain people, you'll be glad if you fight through the discomfort. The positive method is an antidote to the large numbers of empty relationships that often exist on social media. It will help you open the communication in your relationships and create stronger connections with the people who matter most to you.

In terms of including a broad cross-section of people across different parts of your life, don't just take it from me, take it from people who have been through these steps. In an interview with partners at a consulting firm after they created their personal highlight reels, I asked, "What is one piece of advice you would give someone who was just starting the process?" By far, the most frequent response was: *Select a wide range of people from different parts of your social network.*

- Ben from Munich: "Invite people you haven't been in touch with for a while, from all phases of your life."

- Louise from Chicago: "Ask the maximum [number of] people . . . start segmenting through friends, family, peers, supervisors, and team members."

- Jack from England: "Work harder to get more input."

- Martina from Madrid: "Take time to choose those to ask. Try to have the most diverse representation of points of view."

- Nasser from India: "Select a broad spectrum of respondents, especially those who know you as a person and have really seen you."

It's interesting: *Before* going through the highlight reel experience, the eulogy delay makes us want to select as few people as possible. Sometimes, people even shrink back from the positive method altogether.

After going through the process, people see it very differently. Almost like Alice going through the looking-glass, it all changes. After people have read their highlight reels, they understand why it's important to give to, and receive from, as many people as possible, from as many parts of life as possible. You will feel the same.

So go ahead and write down your list. Who do you want to extend some appreciation to? Whose world do you want to brighten? Who are the best people to offer diverse memories for your own personal highlight reel? Who are the people that would speak at your eulogy?

WHEN WE STOP FIGHTING FEAR AND ANXIETY

There are some real benefits to paying it forward, by sending highlight reel stories out to people in your social network. First off, it makes *you* feel more grateful and positive. Second, you are making *other* people feel appreciated. Third, you are modeling the positive method and encouraging people to respond with their stories about you.

But my guess is that, despite everything you've learned about the benefits of this process, there is *still* a large percentage of you hesitating to reach out right now. Many of you may be experiencing some fears and anxieties over taking the next step. And that even as you wrote down the list of people you will reach out to, you experienced some contradictory emotions. You might have felt a few twinges of apprehension about who to include on the list. You might have felt some trepidation about what stories they would include in your highlight reel. I want you to know that all of these feelings are okay.

Hello, eulogy delay! Are you experiencing this force right now, hissing in your ear? "It's too weird, it's too scary, it's too _____ to give and receive these stories." There could be any hundreds of thousands of answers to why we shouldn't take this leap.

Should you listen to it?

When I interviewed the consulting firm partners about this phenomenon, I asked them: "How did you feel when you first found out you were going to ask family, friends, and colleagues to write about you at your best?"

Their answers to this question taught me a few things. First, I learned that the eulogy delay does not hamper everybody. Of the thirty people I interviewed, six said they felt completely comfortable asking for highlight stories. They just felt curiosity and excitement.

But the majority of people felt the force telling them not to reach out to others. In addition to curiosity, many people also felt social discomfort and fear. Overall, there were three major mental obstacles they had to overcome: (1) the anxiety of asking someone to "Tell Me How Great I Am"; (2) the worry that they would be an imposition on others; and (3) the fear of making themselves vulnerable.

Yet, you will soon discover that as we saw in Kumar and Epley's studies, these individuals' concerns were *misplaced*. People in their social network actually *wanted* to share highlight reel stories with them, and, in fact, it was their vulnerability that improved and intensified their relationships.

For example, meet Chloe, who was born in the United Kingdom and now lives in Wisconsin. At twenty years old, she completed her highlight reel as a class exercise at university. Chloe told me: "It was a bit intimidating at first. It was a bit uncomfortable. Like, 'Hey, tell me what you like about me.' But it was also kind of exciting."

So, here you can see the dissonance in Chloe's reactions. Part of her was curious and excited, and part of her was afraid. These two emotions vibrate, and what often happens is that bad emotions are stronger than good emotions, as we saw in chapter 1. Fear usually wins, so we don't reach out. And this is how the eulogy delay beats you.

When later in the interview I asked Chloe how her network *actually* responded to writing highlights about her, she replied, "It seemed like they genuinely enjoyed the process. I had a couple of friends tell me, 'This is actually really fun.' They were happy to do it for me."

In the next few pages, I'm going to share some other "mixed emotion" responses with you and how to overcome the fear of reaching out. The only way forward is when you stop trying to suppress your doubts and allow yourself to move through these feelings of discomfort. I want you to see it is common to experience both curiosity and awkwardness, or even some anxiety, at the beginning of the exercises. It will also be natural to experience raw joy when you read your highlight reel. By hearing people describe these three waves of resistance in their own words, I hope you will empathize with them. You need to see that it is worth the journey.

"TELL ME HOW GREAT I AM"

Fifty-three-year-old Ava from Toronto is a consulting firm partner who focuses on global health practices. I met Ava as a participant in an executive education session in which she completed her highlight reel, and in the session she relayed her reactions to reaching out to others with great insight and precision.

Ava said she felt embarrassed reaching out to her network to write her highlight reel stories. She told me that, by asking her family, friends, and colleagues to write positive stories about her, she thought she was obligating them to do something they didn't want to do. In fact, she was sure of it.

Ava grew up in a family where one of the things you got berated for was "fishing for compliments"—and she felt that this is what she was doing by creating her highlight reel. What Ava learned, however, is that this exercise is far more than asking others to tell us how great we are. Instead, it provides us with the insight needed to recognize our potential, so that we can step into it. And most people who care about us want to help us do this.

Despite Ava's reservations, after she completed her highlight reel she was happily surprised to find that her network *enjoyed* giving her positive feedback:

> *In the end, people actually really were happy to do it. With the right forum, they were delighted to tell me those things. But they wouldn't have told me those things if we hadn't created the catalyst.*

Ava makes a great point here about the process serving as a catalyst for sharing positive memories. It's like the positive method opens a beneficial door that is normally locked. It allows people to extend their full appreciation for you—without it, that door is usually only opened at the end of someone's life.

We can recognize a similar version of this theme emerging with Emma, who lives in Charlotte, North Carolina, and has spent most of her early career putting in long hours to gain partnership in a consulting firm—hours where she often sacrificed time with friends and family.

When I asked how she initially felt about asking for her highlight stories from her network, Emma replied, "It was very exciting.

Intriguing. A little unnerving. We don't usually ask people about the good stuff."

Emma's mixed emotions—moving from excitement and intrigue to unnerved and back again—show how we respond to mixed motives. On the one hand, we want to learn what special qualities our network sees in us, but this desire conflicts with the eulogy delay because we feel uncomfortable asking for it. And that's why we feel the mental dissonance.

Then I asked Emma how people *responded*—in other words, were the people she asked okay with providing stories? She replied, "For the vast majority it felt like they wanted to do it. Because I would do the same. Any of those people, if they had asked me I would've done the same."

Emma is one of those career-focused people who achieved her career goals at a relatively young age. After reading her highlight reel, she told me she wondered what all the fuss was about. Experiencing this wave of appreciation and positivity from her friends and family's stories inspired Emma to invest a little more of her time and energy developing nonwork relationships, which made her life more fulfilling than just gaining material success.

This is why the positive method can be a major improvement in how we interact with each other in society. People *want* to share these stories with each other, once they have a platform to share them.

"I AM AN IMPOSITION"

Forty-nine-year-old Sophia was an extremely bright consulting firm partner from Chicago who took one of my business classes a few years back. She was poised and participated in classroom debates with great confidence. In her team projects, I watched her taking the lead with ease and without an ounce of shyness when it came to making sure everyone did their share of the work. And I admired how she showed such appreciation to the members in her group when they contributed.

Yet, when it came time for her to complete her highlight reel for my class, Sophia told me she felt like she was creating a big imposition by asking for positive stories from her community. While it might be easy to expect someone like Sophia to approach this assignment with the same energy and confidence she brought every-day into the classroom with her peers, she almost skipped the project altogether because she said it felt as if she was asking too much—as if asking to borrow money or their car.

What made it harder for Sophia was that the stories she was asking for were all positive. She was used to getting, and even ask-ing for, critical feedback. In her mind, that was okay because she believed that learning about her limitations could help her improve. But asking for *positive* feedback? She said, "I kind of felt like it was a bigger ask . . . In terms of appreciation and all of that, it just isn't something that I normally would do."

So Sophia almost didn't do it. But since the highlight reel was going to be the focus for a class she was taking (mine!), she decided to think of it as a "social experiment." She would just try it and see what happened. And she was surprised to learn that the people she asked did not see it as a problem at all. As Sophia said, "I definitely felt like it was an imposition. But when I talked to my brother, afterward, he thought it was really cool. They all thought it was kind of interesting."

I hear this same reaction again and again—people think they are imposing on others, but then learn that others liked sharing the stories and the gratitude. Check out Oscar from Stockholm, who felt the weight of fear about reaching out to his community because he thought it was asking too much of other people. Oscar told me, "It scared the shit out of me. Honestly . . . I was actually pushing myself quite a bit to reach out to them and it was clearly outside my comfort zone."

Afterward, when I asked Oscar whether he thought his initial fears about imposing were warranted, he responded, "No, they absolutely loved writing. I had several of them coming back to me before I'd gotten the report asking, 'Can I tell you what I wrote?'

And I think a lot of them felt honored to have been asked to share their thoughts."

The eulogy delay not only holds us back from understanding our impact on other people, but it also makes us shy away from developing better, richer relationships in life.

"I DON'T ENJOY FEELING VULNERABLE"

For many people, the resistance to asking for highlight reel stories is about making themselves vulnerable. Let me introduce you to Gabriela, who grew up in Medellin, Colombia. Gabriela is someone who has a long history of working hard, overcoming tough obstacles in her life, and doing it all with an incredible amount of grit.

When Gabriela was thirteen, she had a serious horseback riding accident. For two months, she had to lie completely flat on her bed, not even able to turn. It wasn't clear if she was going to be able to walk again. Today, as a mom of a thirteen-year-old, Gabriela can't imagine what her parents must have felt during those two months. But she can remember how *she* dealt with it. She said, "I honestly think that's one of my best-self moments, really. I tap into that and think, 'If I could deal with that, I can deal with anything.'" Gabriela had all her homework sent to her from school, although her principal said she didn't need to complete any schoolwork while she was recovering. She also watched tons of American cable on TV and taught herself how to speak English.

Learning English was a big piece to her future, as she went on to earn a master's in international relations and economics and became a partner in a huge American consulting firm. Eventually, Gabriela started her own consulting firm in Latin America, which she grew and sold twelve years later.

When Gabriela decided to create her personal highlight reel, I asked her how she felt about reaching out to her social network. She said, "I had two reactions. The first one was I was very excited and interested in it because I also have a professional and academic interest in these topics. So, I thought, *This is going to be really interesting*. But then Gabriela also felt the force of the eulogy delay, making her anxious:

> *I thought,* Perhaps it would make sense to ask these people. But perhaps I don't want to. *So, there's a little bit of fear there too. Even though you know that they're writing about you at your best—it's not about criticism or anything like that—it felt very intimate and it made me feel vulnerable.*

Gabriela makes an important point. Some of the dissonance that many people feel stems from the fact that, in order to give and receive these positive memories, you are making yourself vulnerable. You are sharing, and asking for, something personal that is usually kept private, due to the eulogy delay. It is ironic that this vulnerability is exactly what will improve your relationship and increase your trust within the relationship. But before getting to that point, the vulnerability can be frightening, even when you are someone as independent and successful as Gabriela. No matter who you are, we all experience some degree of fear of putting ourselves out there.

In the end, the courage pays off. Reflecting on the resistance she felt about reaching out to her network, Gabriela said, "I don't think it should be that way, and that's one of the lessons I took away from this whole exercise."

It is natural to worry about reaching out to your social network. While these fears are unfounded, this doesn't mean that they are not somehow legitimate feelings. When we attempt to break through the social barriers around the eulogy delay we can feel a wave of emotions that are a bit uncomfortable and even intimidating at first. But both the quotes and the empirical studies show how we reliably overestimate the awkwardness and imposition, and we underestimate how positive the experience will be.

Once people complete their highlight reel, they are definitely glad they overcame their doubts. As Gabriela told me when I asked her what advice she would give to someone starting out on their highlight reel: "Open yourself to the possibility of understanding how you have impacted and shaped the world around you, and how this understanding can motivate you going forward to be happier, more impactful, and more you."

Here's what a few others had to say:

- Oscar: "Have the courage to ask as many people as possible! You will get to know sides of yourself that you only thought your role models have."

- Ava: "Be open to the process and allow yourself to be a bit vulnerable—it will pay back in spades . . ."

- Rhee: "It is good to discover your best self through the eyes of others."

Once you are on the other side of the appreciation jolt, you can recognize how the eulogy delay affects you and why it shouldn't hold you back. If you find yourself resisting the process of reaching out to your network, push yourself! You'll be glad you persevered.

As Timothy, a typically modest British student in one of my classes, told me after reading his highlight reel, "Initially, I did not want to participate in this method. It was a slice of hell for me to ask friends and family for these stories. And yet they wrote so much; they were so generous with their time and energy. I am filled with gratitude. This report is like receiving twenty-five gifts."

You are now armed with the tools you need; it's time to get started.

WHAT SHOULD I WRITE?

At this point you have a large, diverse list of people who you can share some gratitude with and who can offer you insights about you at your best. Now, pick just *one* of the people on your list. Perhaps for starters, choose the person you feel the most gratitude toward.

In a way, you already know what to do, from the exercise in chapter 5 when you wrote about your own memories about yourself. It's mostly the same as that, but now you're writing a story about someone else. Describe a specific, concrete memory of a time this person was using their strengths to make their best impact. Every day for the next two weeks, pick one person from your list to write a memory or two about.

I recommend three phases for each person you write about:

First, block off fifteen minutes when you just brainstorm about the person's unique strengths and what you value most about them. Pretend you are going to speak at the person's eulogy, and jot down anything that comes to mind. What made this person so special to you?

- What do they stand for?
- What do they do best?
- What is unique about them?
- How do they make you feel?

When I started writing this book, I was helping create a highlight reel for Ingrid, who is the operating officer at the company I helped create, Essentic. I reflected on Ingrid's unique strengths and how—to me—she stands for turning dreams into realities. When Ingrid is at her best, she makes me feel heard. She is very direct in speaking with me about issues, because I can be overly optimistic at times and sometimes I need to be reined in. She makes me feel like I can trust that things will get done, on time and without problems. So far, these are not specific stories; these are just the feelings and ideas that come to mind when I think about Ingrid's contributions.

Second, it's time to get specific. Let your mind wander as you consider some detailed times when you can remember this person doing what they do best. Dredge your memories for a few specific times that this person was using their character traits, skills, and interests to make a great impact. Maybe you have some memories from the last few years or weeks, while other events happened long ago. As you are brainstorming, jot down a few notes and ideas to choose from. Don't try to write up whole stories yet.

After you have a strong list of possibilities, pick one of these instances and spend about fifteen minutes writing about the event in detail. You can, of course, write up and send several of your memories, but just start with one. Savor the moment as you write about it. Replay the memory in your mind.

You'll find it helpful to start your story off with the phrase, "I remember a time when . . ." And then take the memory from there.

You're going to get out of this what you put into it. You have seen the scientific evidence showing the power of these gratitude letters. Here is some additional advice as you write about your memory.

People don't want to simply be praised—they want to act in ways that are *praiseworthy*. So, as you write, stay away from generalities ("you're so smart" or "you're great with kids") even if they are true. Replay the memory in your mind to get to the specifics. Write about the peculiarities and details of the situation. Include gritty elements of the event that you remember. For example, it would be possible to write, "You always make me feel special." Which is nice, but also vague. Or instead you might write, "From my earliest memories, you were right by my side, taking me on walks through the miniature golf course near our house, preparing my odd lunch requests for cheddar and mayo sandwiches, and sneaking me Almond Joy candy bars away from the gaze of my mom." The second would give the person more of a buzz, because the details and specifics let them relive the memories.

Write directly to the person who will receive the story. This is not for their boss. This is not for their resume. This is for them only to read. So use the pronoun "you"—you aren't talking about "him" or "her."

Remember, human brains are built for stories and our stories about our life experiences are the building blocks to self-construction. So write about this event as a story, not just a collection of facts.

Have a beginning (here was the setting), a middle (here's what you did; here's who was affected), and an end (here is how your contributions solved a problem; here is how your contributions made me feel). This will make a stronger impact on the person.

No story has to be perfect, of course. Make it sincere, but most importantly make it your own. Here is an example of a story I wrote for Ingrid:

I remember a time when you were telling me about your daughter Lizzie getting married. You arrived to find lots of the basics were not sorted out—things like the music and the seating. Basic things that are necessary for a good party. As you were telling me how you helped Lizzie get things sorted, it dawned on me that this is what you do for us at Essentic. You take all the good ideas and good intentions and make them into a reality of operating a business. I know it is not easy to accomplish these realities, but you make it seem easy. As you were telling me about the wedding, what I realized is that your ability to see the logistics and the necessary steps comes naturally to you, when it does not to others (like me!). I saw how you really push yourself to make things happen—to make visions into reality. You connect with clients to help them understand what we do. You took ideas and brought a functional website to life, working tirelessly with Steve to make sure the site is working. You use empathy to help contributors who are confused and need direction. I'm thinking about how, early on, you formalized Essentic with the accountants and lawyers and the government. I am very impressed not only that you do all this, but also that you have a unique ability to make it seem easy. I think Lizzie is lucky to have a mom like you, and I know I am lucky to know you!

Third, send your stories out. Here is a starter note that you can edit, telling people how much you appreciated reflecting on these special moments of connection between you and them. Using your own ideas and language, write something like:

Based on a book I've been reading called Exceptional, *I've been thinking about ways I can improve my relationships and my impact. I don't know if you know this, but you are an important person in my life. I want to share some memories with you about when I've seen you at your best. Then, if you are willing, I'd love to learn about a few times when you saw me making my best impact.*

I can remember a time when . . . [put the story you wrote right here].

The more memories you write about each person, the more they may write about you. The more energy and love you put into their stories, the more they are likely to put into your stories. I just wrote three stories for a friend last week, and from beginning to end I spent about sixty-five minutes across two days. (I put them away for a day, and then went back and edited.)

The evidence suggests that the people in your network will feel an "appreciation jolt" when they read your stories. They will feel good learning about how they have made a positive impact. They will feel gratitude and an urge to give back. That's how the emotion of gratitude creates upward spirals, and it's why you two will become closer after this exercise.

Remember, highlight reels are not about "tell me how great I am." They are about giving a gift to people who are important to you and gathering information to understand how other people perceive you, and receive you, at your best. This "learning mindset" is much better for breaking through the force of the eulogy delay, because the focus is on learning and improving, and not wallowing in praise.

If you make it a priority, you can do this for so many people in your life. Create free joy for you and for them! If you make a goal to do one a day for two weeks, the research suggests you will become a happier human being.

GATHER YOUR STORIES BEFORE READING

Here is some strong advice that may seem counterintuitive: Do not read the stories that people send back to you right away. And definitely don't read your stories as they come dribbling in, one by one. Wait until you have gathered a whole collection of them.

I know that this advice *will be difficult to take*. It will be so tempting to just read them, because it will take a while for your social network to respond to you with their memories. But to experience the positive trauma that we discussed in chapter 4, you want to read them all together. As Ava from Toronto reported:

> *It felt very intense, because it all came at once. When you put it all together, that's when the magic happens. I actually think that's the power of this—a force that just hits you in a much deeper, more meaningful way than if you got it in pieces.*

Ava is right.

Remember we talked about the power of an "appreciation jolt" that can help you rethink your life story? Well, reading the memories as they trickle in diffuses this effect. Especially if you read them on your phone. On a crowded bus. A huge value of the highlight reel comes from the jolt you get when you experience all the feedback at once.

So, to get the power of the appreciation jolt, you're going to wait until you get a critical mass of stories. That might take several weeks, or even months. And it may take a bit of gentle reminding. But when you get enough of them—I'd say ten stories as a minimum—it's time to read the next chapter where I explain *how* to read your highlight reel, so you can get the most out of this experience.

CHAPTER 7

Discover Your Best Impact

I t's finally time to read and work through your highlight reel. By now you have written your three stories about yourself. You also feel positive after writing gratitude letters to people you value in your social network. You probably have already had a few people tell you how happy they are that you reached out to them. And many people have sent stories to you. You have at least ten stories from different parts of your social network. You have created your own living eulogy.

You might be asking, "What if I haven't done the whole process, yet? What if I am just reading the book through this time?"

You can still read on. No alarms will sound. But this chapter *will* make a lot more sense once you have completed your highlight reel. If you haven't yet, hopefully the following pages will inspire you to go back and complete the full process.

There are two elements to working through your highlight reel. First, this chapter will teach you *how* to read these stories to help you get the most out of them. Trust me, it matters a lot how you read your highlight reel.

The second element will be covered in the next chapter, and is all about the thoughts and emotions that you might experience as you read your stories. What you will learn within the next two chapters is based on my findings over the last five years of personally debriefing more than five thousand people who have created their highlight reels, and the qualitative and quantitative data I have gathered with the help of Essentic.

HOW TO READ YOUR HIGHLIGHT REEL

Give your highlight reel the respect that it deserves. It's kind of a big deal. It's possible your network has never talked with you about these stories before, and you may not hear this kind of transparent positive feedback from your community again in this lifetime. Make some time and choose the right space. Your personal highlight reel is not the sort of thing that you want to "skim through." You'll want to allow room for the stories to breathe. You'll want to savor the memories that people took the time to share with you.

In terms of time, an hour should do it. Fifteen minutes will not be enough. In our time-famine world, lots of people I've worked with allocate fifteen minutes. They have either regretted it or have been surprised by how much time actually passed as they experienced their highlight reel. As Gary, a senior leader in a beer brewing and packaging plant in Northern England, told me, "I sat down thinking it was going to be a ten-minute read. It ended up being fifty minutes. It was way more emotional than I expected. I walked out of the room feeling humanized."

In terms of *where* to read the report, find a quiet place where you won't be disturbed or distracted. Don't do it on a busy bus, or in a bar surrounded by other people, or when hanging out with friends.

The goal on the first reading is to just let the stories wash over you and not worry about how you look to other people, which is why reading them alone is ideal. Your first read-through is all about reliving these moments in the stories. That can be hard when others are around because we often feel like we need to hide our emotions, when in fact what we need to be doing is *experiencing* our emotions. Immersing ourselves in the memories and the experience is how we create transformative positive trauma.

As you probably have noticed from the stories throughout the book, many people have strong emotional reactions when they read their reports, especially the first time. And most people actually cry or tear up. That's why it's important to set aside some time in a private space. It is interesting how many people cry, because these are not sad memories. But they are often emotional, and you don't want to have to explain anything to other people yet.

I was a department chair at London Business School when I first read my highlight reel. After reading a story from a high school friend about an event that happened long ago, I felt like my chest was rearranging itself. There was something bittersweet in recalling a memory from all those years ago laid out in my friend's own words. And then as I read the next story from my sister, I noticed big tears dropping onto my report. I didn't feel sad, but I found myself crying and a little overwhelmed. I was surprised by the strength of my reaction.

As department chair, I usually kept my door open. But I remember going over and not only shutting the door, but locking it, so that I could read my report and take in everything without being concerned about interruptions. Reading my highlight reel took me to a very different emotional place than I'd experienced before, which can be hard for other people to understand if they have never experienced it.

Since that first time I read my own highlight reel, I have learned that many other people are also surprised by how emotional it is to read their stories. For example, remember Louise from Chicago? She said, "You cry even though it's just positive things. You just cry because you're definitely not used to hearing positive things. And I think I cried more when I read the stuff from my friends."

Let's pause, for just a minute, to reflect on how interesting it is that hearing about our positive influence is not even normal coming from our *friends*. I felt the same way Louise did. I was really surprised, and touched, about how many wonderful stories my friends had to share with me, but apparently were not going to share with me until I opened this door for them.

Gabriela from Colombia, the consulting firm partner who had the horse accident as a child, also felt very moved when reading her stories. She said, "I cried like a baby for an hour, which is not something that I spend time doing. So that was quite interesting. My emotional response was huge."

This emotional reaction was similar across men and women from all age groups and cultures. Many university students also mentioned strong emotions as they read their highlight reels. Ron, the journalism student who you may recall almost dropped his class to avoid reaching out to his network, wrote: "All in all, I loved this exercise. I was annoyed at having to collect all these stories, but I am so happy I did. I cried while reading them, and I am sure I will cry every time I need to see them to boost my spirits."

Tracey, the actress and economics student whose stories centered on her compassionate nature (like helping her sister when she wet her pants in kindergarten), said, "I did not expect me to completely break down and start bawling multiple times reading the stories. There are certain stories that really opened wounds that never fully healed and reminded me of the struggle of how I overcame them. There are also stories that made me laugh and cry because I did not know that these people thought of me like that."

The reason many of us cried or had such powerful reactions is because these stories are full of so much love, appreciation, and positivity. They show us how we have grown, and they reveal our gifts. And in many ways, they make it impossible to ignore our potential because these letters show us in concrete ways all the good we are capable of.

Now, set aside some time and go ahead with reading your highlight reel.

LOCATING THEMES ACROSS YOUR HIGHLIGHTS

Okay, so on your first read-through of your collection of stories you might have experienced some stimulating and strong emotions. Let that sink in. Then, perhaps after a day or so, you might feel motivated to work through each story again. Not only to savor them again as a gift, but also to start looking for themes and commonalities. Many people find it useful, for example, to make a note of which stories connected or resonated with them the most.

To get the biggest benefit out of your highlight reel, and to discover how you can continue to make your best impact, I recommend that you carefully analyze each story during your next read-through. The goal is to create a more cognitive trail of what you are learning from them. So, as a first step, take some time to identify and capture specific key words and phrases that each writer puts in their story to you. Whether you are working digitally or on paper, you could do this by highlighting words in the actual stories that grab you. Like me, you may prefer to write these key words on a separate digital document so you can easily cut and paste the words.

In many cases, no one word in a story really captures the overall meaning or point of the story, but using your own words, try to distill the essence of each memory—write down what key idea about you stands out. What do you think the person is trying to convey by choosing that specific memory? What are they trying to tell you? Capture the word or phrase that best describes the essence of each story for *you*.

For example, one of the people who wrote a highlight for me was a former PhD student that I advised when I was a professor at the University of North Carolina:

> *Your interest is in colleagues as people and not just as a means for getting work done. For example, I think of the times that you made time to have coffee with me and gave me career advice, you responded to my email about MBA teaching concerns, you called to congratulate me on an*

award I received, you brought your family to meet mine, and you shared your own external interests with me (family, drawing, travel, etc.). I would like to say this behavior is the norm for advisor relationships, but I've found that sincere and enduring interest in a student's development as both academic and as a person is not standard. Thank you!

First, "Thank you back!" After all this time, I still really appreciate it. It actually still makes me so happy and proud when I read it. When I first read this story, the core theme or strength that leapt out for me was "I take a sincere interest in other people." So I added this to my key words document.

After you have worked through each story and captured the core idea, start to look for themes, similarities, and recurring concepts that emerge across all the stories and contributors. Note this on the same key words page you've created, or you could create a new page entitled "My Consistent Highlights." The point, here, is finding central ideas that several people expressed in their memories. This is eventually going to help you identify your core strengths. And even though everyone will have their own unique experiences with you, and will write about different events, they might see your most valuable contributions in similar ways.

Here are four specific exercises you can do to further identify consistent themes:

1. **Look for linkages between the highlight reel stories you wrote about yourself and those from your social network.** I got a boost of energy, personally, from seeing how often people's memories of me at my best showed how I am sincere and honest when talking with other people. This was something that I noticed about myself from my own stories.

2. **Review the cohesiveness in stories between different parts of your social network.** Do you find there are more similarities or differences between work and nonwork? Between family

and friends? Between parents and friends? Obviously, the more people you have stories from, the better this analysis will be.

3. **Create your own word map or word cloud of what you learned from your highlight reel.** You might try doing this visually, so that you put the most common and consistent key phrases in the middle, and then work your way out from the middle. You could write in smaller letters as you move out from the center. Other people may wish to complete this on a spreadsheet, where you label each story, put the consistent key words and phrases in a column, and put the source of the story on the rows.

4. **Try copying and pasting all your stories into a word cloud app and see what major and minor themes emerge.** It is interesting to compare how the app's word cloud matches with what you personally thought after reading and diagnosing the stories. You also could try putting the highlight reel stories that you wrote (about yourself) into the app and see what emerges. It can be informative to compare the results from your own stories to the results from the stories your network sent you.

Take this research you've done on the stories that people have shared with you and add it to your highlight reel folder. You will want to refer back to it later in this chapter.

GETTING ARTSY

So far, your "story analysis" has focused on language and words. But words are hardly the only way to gather insights. When I help people debrief their experience with their highlight reel, I often suggest they use art. As in, pastels or painting or drawing or clay—and sometimes Legos! Why? Because art allows people to express themselves in ways that words do not. Art also leaves a physical trace that acts as a faster-than-words reminder of your best self. You can hang it up, or take a picture of it and make it your background image on your computer when you're done.

★ *Represent Yourself with Art* ★

Get yourself a large piece of paper and a box of crayons (or pastels, colored pencils, paints, clay, Legos, or whatever medium you like). Now, select the highlight reel story that resonated with you the most. For many people, there is usually one or two stories that encompass or "embody" your entire highlight reel in a meaningful way. After you have selected that story, spend twenty minutes using any art that you wish to represent it.

Research suggests that the act of drawing and representing things encourages a more seamless integration of the memories in our brains. The act of drawing or representing the memory weaves it deeper in your mind and makes it easier to recall. Studies show that any time you add an additional form of processing into your learning, it establishes the memory more than just the original stimulus itself would have.

Sometimes people actually draw the story in a "realistic" way, to make it look like the memory itself, as best they can remember it. But the goal does not have to be "realism" at all. Another goal can be to examine what your subconscious produces when you set it free. What colors does this story make you think of? What shape? What texture? Put that into your drawing and see what you learn.

Once you've completed your drawing, you could then get together with a friend, ideally someone who also has been or is going through the positive method. Or perhaps someone who wrote one of your stories for you. Whoever it is, share your representation with that person. Explain your art to them: Tell them how you think and feel about your representation. Talking about your work with someone else lets you process what you've learned even more and also helps you "own" your best self by committing to it verbally. When you are done, add this artwork to your highlight reel folder.

IDENTIFYING YOUR SIGNATURE STRENGTHS

Using the insights that you have gained so far in this chapter (key word research, pinpointing consistent themes, and your artistic rendition), in this final stage you are going to learn how to identify your *signature strengths*.

Signature strengths are your unique qualities and tendencies that make up your best possible self. They are your superpowers—the strongest and most prominent of all your strengths, the most standout qualities that are central to your identity. I don't like to get hung up on terminology, but you could also think of them as *character strengths* or *core strengths*.

Don't think of your signature strengths in terms of a specific expertise. We are not necessarily talking here about "accounting" or "writing" or "public speaking." Your signature strengths are usually broader than that. They are more expansive than any particular role, job, or relationship. They are more about your core capacities for thinking, feeling, and behaving in ways that can bring positive impact into your life and the lives of others.

Marcus Buckingham, author and motivational speaker you met back in the introduction, put it like this:

> *A strength is more than a skill—a technical proficiency like working with numbers or using a certain kind of tool. A strength is a broader aptitude you have or build for solving problems, getting things done, influencing people, or building relationships.*

As you prepare to articulate your own signature strengths based on your highlight reel, think beyond single words (such as "smart" or "organized"). Instead, think of signature strengths as the natural way you act when are at your best. Laura Morgan Roberts, who designed the Reflected Best-Self Exercise, said the following:

We're not looking for a personality trait or characteristic, like "I am kind." But what we found from our research is that the more compelling descriptions of strengths and best selves are in the form of action orientations. So instead of saying "I am kind," it's saying, for instance, "I show up for people when they need me."

We often find our core strengths hiding in our actions—in how we react to situations, how we treat others, and how we enact our decisions. Just like you can't be summed up in one word or one character trait, your strengths also are intricate and detailed. The more specific you can be in identifying your signature strengths, the more authentic and real this quality will feel, and the easier it will be to embed this in your mind.

ALL SKILLS ARE NOT SIGNATURE STRENGTHS

Just because you're *good* at something doesn't always mean you actually *like* that activity. Even when you are great at a certain skill, it is not a signature strength if you do not find joy in exercising that skill. I might once have been good at thinking about statistics, for example, because it was a big part of my PhD training, and because I publish scientific papers using statistics. However, I don't actually like statistics very much. I definitely prefer working with colleagues who enjoy running the analyses. So, statistics and detecting trends within data are not part of my signature strengths.

A clear sign of a skill that is not a signature strength is when performing it drains you, instead of energizing you. I'll never forget one participant in a class I was running named David who taught me all about this. The group had read their highlight reels the night before, and David told us how several of his family and friends had written about his calm, composed demeanor during a recent crisis. They praised his ability to get things done in an emergency. When the class began discussing how to craft their lives around their strengths (which is something you will learn to do in chapter 10), David told us, "I really hope this doesn't mean I need to get myself into more crises. That took years off my life." While it may be helpful for David to know that he keeps cool during a crisis, he also recognized that it is not a signature strength because it is extremely depleting.

None of us should craft a life around activities that drain us. Even if we're good at them.

Your signature strengths sit squarely at the intersection of "I'm good at it" and "I enjoy it." This is exactly what you are trying to identify as you are working through the stories in your highlight reel.

★ *Turn Your Strength into an Action* ★

Take fifteen minutes to review the research you have done on your highlight reel and practice articulating one of your signature strengths as an action orientation (the way you *act,* not a description of your traits). For example, instead of "good with people," I wrote, "I take a sincere interest in other people as one of my signature strengths." Often, you will see your signature strengths emerging in several stories across the span of your life, in different contexts, and with different people.

SIGNATURE STRENGTHS LITMUS TESTS

To help you identify and understand your core strengths, I'm now going to give you a number of questions to consider. These questions are derived from Martin Seligman's positive psychology research, where he describes the "hallmarks" of strengths. You might find it helpful to write down or type out your answers. It is also best to sit in a quiet place as your reflect on these questions.

1. **What activities were you already doing as a child that you still like to do now?**

   Obviously, you probably do them much better now, but your signature strengths often have deep roots. We can see them emerging in our early lives, and this can be one way to identify them. Look at any childhood memories that your family and friends wrote about. Combine this with your own memories of when you were a child. For me, reading books and writing stories was something I was much more intrigued by than many of my friends, even as early as seven years old. I can remember in second grade being truly excited to order books from Scholastic during our school book fair, and then spending the summer reading. To this day I still love to read and learn about other cultures and people through books. And as you might have been able to guess from the book you are holding now, I continue to be absorbed with storytelling and writing.

2. **What activities give you an energetic buzz when you are doing them?**

   As you relive the memories that people shared with you in your stories, some of them may make you recall a sense of energy and excitement. Think carefully about what you were doing in those memories, because these activities were very likely calling on your signature strengths. For me, when I am meeting new people and trying to connect with them, I feel like it "wakes me up." It gives me energy. So, some of what you are looking for here, across your own memories and those other people shared with you, is a feeling of excitement, joy, and enthusiasm while using the strength. It is empowering to use a strength that overlaps both "I'm good at it" and "I like it." That's why you feel invigoration rather than exhaustion while using it: The more you use it, the more energy you have. This will become an important key in step 3, when you start to craft new behaviors and experiments around your signature strengths.

3. **Are there some activities that you never need to put on your "To Do" list?**
You may notice that other people need to remind themselves to do certain tasks that you find yourself pulled toward naturally. And you may notice that you have to tell yourself again and again to complete certain tasks, while other tasks you find yourself doing without any nudge or reminders. For example, it's hard for me to *not* work on this book, whereas I need to create reminders to prepare for administrative meetings (and even then I wait until the last minute). The things that always seem to get done often reveal an underlying signature strength—they are the things we never need to be asked twice to do.

4. **When do you feel most like the "real you"?**
If you look across the stories that people wrote for you, and also go through your own stories and memories, are there any that make you think, *Ahhhh, this feels like the real me when I am doing this.* Chances are that when you are feeling this way you're using your signature strengths. Back in chapter 1, we saw in the research how highlight reels made people feel more authentic, which led to personal resilience. We want to express who we really are through our behaviors and activities; we want to live more authentic lives. The activities that make us feel more like ourselves are often the activities that draw on our signature strengths. Which is why experiencing our highlight reel can make us feel a sense of purpose. The connection

between our best qualities and our authentic selves gives more meaning in our daily lives.

5. **Which activities come naturally to you?**
You may find there are activities in which you have a tendency to excel without exerting a lot of effort. This does not always mean that you find a certain activity "easy," but perhaps there are one or two that come *easier* compared to other activities mentioned in your highlight reel. Can you identify a few from the stories that people sent you?

Here are two hallmarks to look for: First, we often feel *a sense of yearning* or craving to find new ways to use a signature strength. It's almost like we are born "wired" to use certain core strengths, and when we use them nature rewards us with good feelings that make us strive to find other ways to use them. We then find ourselves exercising those skills more often, and in different ways, throughout our lives. Can you identify a few moments when you felt this way within the stories that people sent you? How about in the different areas of your life, work, home, and more?

Second, a *rapid learning curve* is another hallmark. Thinking back across the stories that people wrote about you, and that you wrote about yourself, what are the things that you have picked up quickly, learning them almost effortlessly?

When you are working with a signature strength, a little practice seems to go a long way. You find ways to increase your impact more quickly when you work using these strengths. This is really important, and exciting, because it shows why developing signature strengths is probably a better use of your time than shoring up limitations and deficiencies. Remember Rebecca? We can work long and hard on our deficiencies, exhausting ourselves in the process and feeling bad without making much improvement in how we impact others. Or we can invest in playing to our strengths, and quickly make far greater progress, while feeling better about it.

> ### ★ *Pinpoint Your Signature Strengths* ★
>
> Take thirty minutes, now, to describe your signature strengths using everything you've learned so far. I'd like you to capture as many core strengths that emerge from your highlight reel as possible. Like the practice session on page 119, make sure you articulate your signature strengths as an action orientation. When you are finished with the exercise, put your work in your highlight reel folder.
>
> Once you are done studying the stories your network shared with you, put this inside the folder as well. You will want to keep them safe and continue to revisit them in the future.

TAKE IT FROM THE TOP

One of the most exciting elements of your highlight reel is how unique it is to you. You did not start with a survey asking you about preconceived strengths that you "should" have relative to other people. You did not have to answer "strongly agree" or "strongly disagree" on a numeric rating scale. No, you built your highlight reel "from the ground up" based on personal, intimate stories written by you and people who know you well. And then you used these stories to locate your signature strengths, which ensures that it is completely relevant to you.

That said, there also is an objective approach that complements the work you have done so far. You also can look at your strengths "from the top down." What I mean by this is that you can see how you fit into an overarching, high-level list of common signature strengths, such as the Universal Strengths determined by Martin Seligman and his colleagues. Their research shows that there are twenty-four strengths that are typical across cultures and nations. You and I have all two dozen of these strengths, but we each have them in different degrees. Some are at the top of your signature strengths, while others do not appear as strongly in you. This means that each person has a unique "profile" of strengths, like a fingerprint.

If you'd like, you can take the free survey online to identify your character strengths according to Seligman's research (viacharacter.org). It will rank your strengths and give you information on where you stand. While the test is valid, you may find that the "answer" you get from a top-down survey method is not as personal, detailed, or grounded as what you found from reading your own stories from your network.

But there is a way to bring the two approaches—bottom-up and top-down—together, so that they complement each other. In the following exercise you will match each of your personal stories in your highlight reel with one or more of the twenty-four universal strengths to see which show up most regularly across your stories.

YOUR HIGHLIGHTS AND YOUR UNIVERSAL STRENGTHS

In this first step, take one story at a time and note which of the universal strengths in Seligman's list best describes the theme of that story. Do this for each of the stories that make up your highlight reel. Some stories might show several of these strengths. That's okay too.

Twenty-Four Universal Strengths

Appreciation of Beauty and Excellence: "I recognize, emotionally experience, and appreciate the beauty around me and the skill of others."

Bravery: "I act on my convictions, and I face threats, challenges, difficulties, and pains, despite my doubts and fears."

Creativity: "I am creative, conceptualizing something useful, and coming up with ideas that result in something worthwhile."

Curiosity: "I seek out situations where I gain new experiences without getting in my own or other people's way."

Fairness: "I treat everyone equally and fairly, and give everyone the same chance, applying the same rules to everyone."

Forgiveness: "I forgive others when they upset me and/or when they behave badly toward me, and I use that information in my future relations with them."

Gratitude: "I am grateful for many things and I express that thankfulness to others."

Honesty: "I am honest to myself and to others, I try to present myself and my reactions accurately to each person, and I take responsibility for my actions."

Hope: "I am realistic and also full of optimism about the future, believing in my actions and feeling confident things will turn out well."

Humility: "I see my strengths and talents but I am humble, not seeking to be the center of attention or to receive recognition."

Humor: "I approach life playfully, making others laugh and finding humor in difficult and stressful times."

Judgment: "I weigh all aspects objectively in making decisions, including arguments that are in conflict with my convictions."

Kindness: "I am helpful and empathic and regularly do nice favors for others without expecting anything in return."

Leadership: "I take charge and guide groups to meaningful goals and ensure good relations among group members."

Love: "I experience close, loving relationships that are characterized by giving and receiving love, warmth, and caring."

Love of Learning: "I am motivated to acquire new levels of knowledge, or deepen my existing knowledge or skills in a significant way."

Perseverance: "I persist toward my goals despite obstacles, discouragements, or disappointments."

Perspective: "I give advice to others by considering different (and relevant) perspectives and using my own experiences and knowledge to clarify the big picture."

Prudence: "I act carefully and cautiously, looking to avoid unnecessary risks and planning with the future in mind."

Self-Regulation: "I manage my feelings and actions and am disciplined and self-controlled."

Social Intelligence: "I am aware of and understand my feelings and thoughts, as well as the feelings of those around me."

Spirituality: "I feel spiritual and believe in a sense of purpose or meaning in my life, and I see my place in the grand scheme of the universe and find meaning in everyday life."

Teamwork: "I am a helpful and contributing group and team member and feel responsible for helping the team reach its goals."

Zest: "I feel vital and full of energy, and I approach life feeling activated and enthusiastic."

Then for your next step, once you have categorized each of your stories according to one or two strengths from the preceding list, take fifteen minutes to perform some *top-down* analyses. Which of the twenty-four strengths showed up most frequently in your stories? Circle the one or two signature strengths that are revealed most consistently and prominently in your stories. This exercise allows you to learn how your own personal stories fit into a universal set of general human strengths.

When you have finished with this exercise, put it in your high-light reel folder as a validated, and personalized, reminder of your signature strengths. If you took the online survey, print this and add the results to your folder too.

In this chapter, we developed a structure for *how* to read and interpret your highlight reel so that you get the most out of it. In the next chapter, we will focus on exploring how the highlight reel experience made you feel and the way it affected you. You can compare your own personal reactions with others who have gone through the same process and learn what other people took away from their reports that might also be helpful to you. These reflections will prepare you for stretching into your strengths in the last section of the book.

CHAPTER 8

Hear Your Own Eulogy

E veryone has a different experience when they read their highlight reel. But after talking with and studying thousands and
thousands of people from around the world, I have found
that most are affected in four primary and positive ways: they feel
humility and motivation; they recognize positive blind spots; they
discover the power of their impact; and they feel affirmed about
their identity and their strengths. You might have experienced some
of these feelings more deeply than others, and chances are more than
one of them resonated with you.

Together, these four reactions are at the heart of the appreciation jolt, with each of these feelings pushing us closer to that jolt.
As I described in chapter 4, this is the positive trauma that I hope
can take the place of an *actual* threatening event. Positive trauma
is important because research shows that it leads people to deeper
relationships, feeling more meaning in life, and gives them the motivation to make a bigger difference in the world.

Reading your highlight reel is a little like hearing your own
eulogy, which can be life changing. Just as it helped Alfred Nobel
change his behaviors when he saw how he was perceived by others,

you can gain real insights and motivation from learning which memories and themes other people attach to you.

As you reflect on the way you felt reading your stories, see how you identify with the four experiences described in this chapter. This will help you not only process your own thoughts and emotions surrounding your highlight reel but also increase your awareness of the positive trauma you've created for yourself.

1. HUMILITY, NOT ARROGANCE

When I first introduce the positive method in my classes, I find that many students simply do not believe that reading a highlight reel could lead to humility. Their intuition says the opposite—they assume it would make people conceited and arrogant to hear so much praise about themselves. Can you imagine how the conversation might go explaining this process to an acquaintance who hasn't read *Exceptional*?

> *You:* A bunch of my family, friends, and colleagues just wrote some really nice things about me. I'm going to go read it now.
>
> *Them:* What, spontaneously? They all just happened to simultaneously write nice things about you? You must have some incredible friends.
>
> *You:* Well, no, I asked them to.
>
> *Them:* Wait. You ASKED them to write nice things about you?!
>
> *You:* Right. I asked them to write down their memories of me at my best.
>
> *Them:* Did this also include your weaknesses or areas you could improve?
>
> *You:* No, this is only about me at my best. I'm trying to focus on my strengths.
>
> *Them:* Wow, seems like a kind of lopsided view. Won't it all go to your head?!

Imagine how surprised this person might be if they learned that humility, and not arrogance, is the most common feeling to emerge from highlight reels.

In interview after interview, people describe how their highlight reel made them feel humbled. Take Ben, a single dad of three kids, who lives in Munich. He completed his highlight reel when he came to London Business School to attend a session on best-self activation. Here's how Ben described his experience reading his stories:

> I felt blessed and humbled that people actually took the time to really go back and think about me. I felt that they wanted to give me a little treasure. And it helped me to better understand how I developed over time, and became who I am right now.

This was a typical reaction I heard from mature adults with forty or fifty years of life experience to draw upon. But what about the so-called "snowflake generation"? For a generation supposedly deemed to be more self-centered and less resilient than the rest, maybe a highlight reel might make these young people arrogant and demotivated?

Nope. I heard the same sentiments of humility and gratitude from the college students who reported on their highlight reel experiences. Such as Tracey, who you know from other chapters. She realized through her highlight reel experience that she was her most authentic and exceptional self when she was showing compassion to others, and that it was one of her signature strengths. This was something she enjoyed, whether helping a friend out with a ride to class or being there for her family when they needed it. As she put it, "I am humbled to realize that a time I was seen at my best was a time that I felt at my best and was doing something I cared about most."

Tracey's stories humbled her because they showed how her strengths were lying in plain sight, and her family and friends recognized them in her daily actions. She used to believe that she was never doing enough for others, but when she read about the compassion each person in her community had observed, she was touched. She was humbled to find out that she shined most when doing something she cared deeply about, such as helping the people in her life.

And rather than become complacent, many of the young adults I interviewed also felt motivated to give back and to use their strengths more often. Here is what University of Michigan student Ron said about reading his stories: "I felt inspired and engaged. I'm considering how I can leverage these strengths more." Ron felt empowered and eager to use the organizational skills that his network had revealed as one of his signature strengths. He felt appreciated and more excited than ever to structure and take the lead on group projects, plan weekend getaways with his friends, and locate events for creative dates with his girlfriend.

Humility and motivation might seem counterintuitive to many outside of the experience. It's easy to imagine someone reading all the positive stories about themselves and saying, "If I'm this good already, then I don't need to improve a thing!"

But when people get insight into their best selves, they become energized to *use* what they learned. Remember Tom from chapter 2, who helped his sixteen-year-old daughter when she was struggling with her epilepsy? Tom was deeply moved and motivated by his daughter's story and his entire highlight reel experience:

> *Do I feel good about what I do as a person, in the world, and with my family? Yes. Am I perfect? Absolutely not. So, hearing about the impact of the things you're doing, I think is just reinforcing that you should do more of that.*

The highlight reel experience is all about helping each other recognize our real potential. Once we see how much we can affect others, it helps us strive to become our best more often. The road to becoming that exceptional version of ourselves lights up.

★ *Tune In to the Motivation* ★

Now that you are finished reading your own stories, pause for a moment to look inside yourself. Take ten minutes to write down some of your own personal reactions to the report.

What did *you* feel? What did you experience personally? Do *you* feel arrogant, or do you feel humbled by this experience? Do you feel more complacent, or do you feel more energized and motivated?

2. POSITIVE BLIND SPOTS

A second theme that emerges strongly in my interview data, again and again, is that people discover positive blind spots about themselves. Even though they already know themselves well, this process can reveal new information about their strengths, or a strength they didn't even know they had.

As one person asked me after reading his highlight reel, "How is it that I have lived with myself for so long—over forty years—and not known this was something people valued about me?" This harkens back to Coma Dave, from chapter 2, who was surprised to learn that people appreciated some of his qualities and traits in a way that he himself didn't appreciate.

We often wind our way through life keenly aware of our weaknesses, but without a highlight reel we are often "flying blind" when it comes to recognizing our best features.

As we discussed earlier in the book, many of us drive ourselves full-tilt upon our limitations, to the point of self-cruelty in our lives. And as you've seen in the experiences of others throughout the book, we often focus on our negatives and overlook our strengths. The eulogy delay keeps people from sharing positive information about each other, which keeps us trapped in this weakness-focused mentality—unless we create the opportunity to see our strengths as we did with the highlight reel. Remember what Coma Dave said, after reading his eulogies: "I found myself thinking, *I'm actually a pretty good dude.*"

Oscar from Stockholm, who you may recall had been scared to ask people for stories of him, felt surprised when he at last read his highlight reel. Oscar knew he could be conceited and irascible, and in fact it was something he worried about and sometimes even disliked about himself. "Pardon my language," he told me sheepishly, "but sometimes I can be a cocky son of a bitch." But Oscar was touched to discover that his network appreciated him for having "a strong point of view" and liked that he actually shared his concerns when he had them.

He was happily surprised to find that some very important relationships in his life found his confidence and outspoken nature to be invaluable. It was part of what made him exceptional, to them. When people described how much they appreciated these traits in Oscar, it motivated him to accept this as a strength rather than a weakness and helped expand his opinion of himself.

Of course, Oscar obviously has to be sure to use this strength in the right way to make his best impact. As we'll see in chapter 10, it is possible to use our strengths unintelligently and hinder ourselves.

Let me tell you a little more about Ben, from earlier. Growing up, Ben was the youngest of four. Both his mom and dad were gone a lot, working hard to build up the two pharmacies they opened. While Ben enjoyed the care of a big family, he also felt a lot of competition with his brothers and sisters for attention:

> *My siblings seem to be much more intelligent than I am. They had very good marks in school. They were all studying medicine. I felt like, "Oh, I should be able to achieve the same thing." But at the same time, I was maybe not at*

their level because I was a little bit lazy as the youngest. And
maybe not getting the same discipline from my parents.

Ben went his own route, away from medicine and into business. After earning his master's degree at Stockholm School of Economics, he was recruited to join an investment bank in London, and then after a few years was hired by a different investment bank to work in New York. Ben described these jobs like this: "You jump into a shark pond and try to survive as long as possible." Ben recognized, over time, that his strengths were more about connecting with people, and less on analytics. So he moved from banking into consulting, and over two decades has been promoted to partner.

Years later Ben created his highlight reel, and what he found most interesting is that many of the stories by his non-workplace contributors focused on his curiosity. The memories that people shared from across his life showed this strength as central to his being, and this really resonated with him. Ben even painted one of his stories about his curiosity as a signature strength when we did some art in a debrief session. Unfortunately, curiosity was not a tendency that he was bringing into the workplace. Not a single work colleague even mentioned it. Ben said this when he realized this positive blind spot:

> *This was a little bit surprising, because [my friends and family] were describing strengths which I forgot about, or I was not really leveraging in my professional life. One thing, which I was not aware of, is they described me as someone who was always trying to find out new things, or was trying to invent things. I was always trying to excite people around me with new things, and they enjoyed this curiosity. They remembered a teenager or a young kid who was full of ideas, who was very excited and curious about things.*

What bothered Ben was how he was no longer drawing on his insatiable curiosity and playfulness in his job. He was not bringing the best part of himself to work. Ben decided this was something that he could address by experimenting with ways to start using his strengths in his everyday tasks at work, something you will learn about in step 3. Ben's story shows us how we can make important changes in our lives once we discover our positive blind spots, and once we have, we can find more happiness and meaning by using our gifts more intentionally.

★ *Illuminate the Good* ★

As you contemplate your own stories, take ten minutes to write down some of your own personal reactions. Did your own high-light reel illuminate any positive blind spots that others valued more than you? What surprised you about your own strengths?

3. A FISH DOESN'T KNOW THAT IT'S WET

We just saw how one type of blind spot is learning new information about our strengths. A second type of blind spot is realizing the *impact* of our strengths. As you read your report, you might be surprised by the "little things" that people took the time to remember and write about. Sometimes people will isolate a memory of something "small" that you did years ago—perhaps decades ago—and describe in detail how it affected them. Perhaps you hardly even remembered some of the events that your friends, family, and colleagues wrote about.

For example, remember Ava from Toronto, who initially felt she was "fishing for compliments" by creating her highlight reel? Ava reported feeling surprised by her highlight reel and the impact she had on others. Ava already knew she had good social skills, like most people in her network and in the consulting profession. What she did not know, until her highlight reel, is that people saw the *level* of her social and inclusion skills as something that was unique to her. She didn't fully understand how it made her exceptional:

> It was an "aha" moment for me where I said, "I guess everyone doesn't do that." For me, that's normal, and I don't know anything else. But it was this moment of, "I guess this is unique, some of the things that I do." And I didn't appreciate it. Up until that moment.

Ava seemed to enjoy making others feel included and engaging with people in a way that made them feel heard and important. It came naturally to her and really differentiated her, yet it took the highlight reel experience for her to recognize just how she made the people in her life feel special and energized when she interacted with them. As we will discuss in chapter 10, Ava's highlight reel helped her realize that she could—and should—find ways to use this signature strength to make an even bigger impact in the future.

Forty-two-year-old Liam, born in Mumbai and now living in Sydney, also recognized a blind spot when he read his stories. Like Ava and many others, however, the blind spot was not about his strengths, but in the specific ways they were felt by others. He knew that he was good at staying goal-focused, and getting other people excited about reaching shared goals, but he thought that was just "normal":

> There wasn't any new information there. It's probably more about reminding me of something that had happened—that had obviously been meaningful to the person—that I had forgotten about or hadn't thought about in a long time. So it was like a rediscovery more than it was a discovery.

How can this be, that we forget so many of our actions that were so meaningful to others—actions that they remember for years, even decades? It's because our signature strengths make our natural action tendencies seem simple, to us. Acting out our strengths, whether it be Ava's inclusive social skills or Liam's ability to get people excited about a vision of the future, often doesn't seem like a big deal, to us, so we dismiss it as "easy" or "nothing." We all possess strengths that come naturally and almost effortlessly to us. In fact, we are so used to these strengths that they just become the air that we breathe and sometimes we completely miss the profound positive effect they can have.

Have you ever heard the phrase "A fish doesn't know that it's wet"? It doesn't know, because it has never experienced life outside water. Just like we don't know of life outside our strengths. Because our strengths come easily to us, we may even *devalue* them as "simple behaviors." But they have a big influence on the people we care about. And it can feel really motivating to learn about this impact. It can make us yearn to use these strengths to make an even bigger difference in the lives of the people we love and the work that we do.

As we learned in chapter 1, seeing our impact on others can make life feel more meaningful—more purposeful. For example, remember Sophia from Chicago, who said that asking for positive stories felt like asking to borrow someone's family car? Two of Sophia's signature strengths are her fearlessness when it comes to complexity and making the best decisions when things are chaotic and messy. She knew that this was something she was good at, but she was not aware of the way this skill impacted others. Here is what she said about reading her highlight reel:

> There were things that I knew, but I never actually had that vision of how they impacted other people. It was just who I am and what I did. I didn't think it was in any way special. That's what kind of struck me. I would say, 75% of what was in there were just things I did because that's what I thought was the right thing to do. To see that that made a difference changed how I thought about some of those everyday moments, and how important they are. The only thing that was really surprising was how these little

*moments that I had not paid attention to had made such a
big impact on people.*

On one hand, Sophia already knew about the strengths that
appeared in her highlight reel. But on the other hand, it surprised
her how *meaningful* other people found her behaviors when she
used those strengths, even when they seemed small—and possibly
forgettable—to her.

Antônia from Brazil, who you may recall from chapter 3, found
a deeper sense of confidence by learning about the impact her
strengths had on others.

Antônia came from a poor background in São Paulo, and after
overcoming numerous hardships had accomplished many successes
in her life, including an MBA from the University of Chicago and
partnership in a global consultancy. Despite all the good she had
done in her past, she had begun to feel unsure of herself when her
new role as managing director was not off to a great start. It wasn't
until reading her uncle's story in her highlight reel that she was
reminded how powerful her actions could be:

> *I don't remember the event. But [my uncle] said, "Antônia,
> there was a time you were just thirteen years old and we
> were together. And the family was fighting about a topic and
> you were the one who came up with a solution. You said,
> 'You guys should do this.' You put everybody on a path. You
> solved the problem, and the family was okay." And I don't
> remember it, but he does.*

Antônia told me that even though she knew she was a good
problem-solver, sometimes she doubted how effective she was. When
she created her highlight reel, she was not in a great place because
she was still adjusting to her new role at work. Antônia told me
that reading her stories meant so much to her because she had, in
her words, been "throwing her past away" as she struggled to cope
with the new job. When her highlight reel allowed her to relive the

moments that people wrote about, she felt grounded and centered. She was reminded how other people noticed and valued her natural contributions, even those that seemed small to her.

What often surprises people about their highlight reel is how the "little things" that come easily to them touch people far more than the "big things" in life that they prepare and put lots of effort into. Here's how forty-six-year-old Andrew from London described it:

> So this is one of the stories from my wife. Her parents were driving down to our house on Christmas Day, and they live up in the north of England, and they broke down in a service station. So I dropped everything, drove up to pick them up, sorted the car out, and drove them back down to our house so they could spend Christmas evening. I hadn't appreciated how much my wife had appreciated me doing that. I'm welling up just thinking about her story. I hadn't quite appreciated how much I stand out in some of these things.

Andrew was surprised how many of the behaviors people wrote about seemed small to him. He told me, "Most of the stories were little stories. They weren't blockbusters. It was the smaller stuff that I found most surprising and touching." Learning about the impact of his behaviors energized Andrew to help other people even more, and to take time to do more small acts of kindness.

Marcus Buckingham, the writer who has perhaps done more than anyone to get people playing to their strengths, said the following:

> I think deep down, we don't actually think that our unique way of engaging with the world is worth uncovering. And what we need sometimes is someone going, "No, no, no, that's you. That's weird. Like, not everyone does X or does Y." It does take a while for you to accept: "This actually is the way I uniquely engage with the world."

4. SELF-VERIFICATION

Even if there are no surprises in your report, you might gain a sense of peace or warmth if you see that other people "get" you. As we saw in chapter 1, it can make you feel authentic when people see the real you. As Coma Dave said, "It seemed that people understood my interpersonal intensity, my combativeness and my contrarianism, in ways I never thought they could . . . I had concrete, digital evidence that I was understood to the core of my personality."

What is this positive feeling we have when we learn that other people know us for who we really are? Bill Swann, a professor of psychology at the University of Texas, calls this *self-verification*. Swann is referring to our deep, human motive to create a social reality that confirms our self-conceptions. In my own empirical research, I have found that we want others to have accurate reflections of how we see ourselves so that we feel coherence—and we know, deep inside, that coherence is just not sustainable when other people expect more or less out of us than we can deliver. So, it gives our world integrity and stability when others know us for who we really are.

What I have found most interesting about self-verification in the context of highlight reels is the focus on the positive. Our highlight reels give us an interesting lens on being understood and accepted for who we really are, including the darker "shadow side" of our strengths and personality. So, for example, Coma Dave described some of his eulogies as "stories that touched on the thornier aspects of my personality in ways that redeemed them." People saw his inter-personal intensity and combativeness, but they also saw how this led to intense loyalty with friends.

Remember Louise, the unswerving, high-powered partner in a global consulting firm? She described her reaction to her highlight reel this way:

> *There were one or two stories where we had different points of view. So an area where I feel I'm weak, they saw a strength, which was kind of interesting. And maybe this was also more moving because I thought I was not doing that great, and some people saw something different.*

So on one hand, you might expect that Louise is not self-verified, because others saw a strength in something she considered as weakness. But Louise *did* feel self-verified by her highlight reel, because she and her network are seeing different sides of the same underlying tendency, and her network is reminding her why it is a strength.

What Louise perceived as a limitation—that she became anxious about public speaking—her colleagues, friends, and even family saw as a real strength, because she is an excellent communicator who people want to listen to. Louise saw that the problem was she was treating work speeches as "events" that made her anxious because she thought she needed to execute them flawlessly, rather than just a form of communication that she was actually skilled at. The feeling of self-verification is having people across different parts of your life see your tendencies, accept them, and value them—and to do this, they may not always have the exact same viewpoint as you.

This also is why it can feel so reassuring when we see the consistency between *different parts of our social network*. Antônia from São Paulo touched on this, when she said she was heartened by the cohesiveness of the themes that emerged:

> *There was consistency, and the people were so different. Because I asked family, friends, and people that worked with me and became friends, but from different times and different places. That really made a difference to me, and that's why it was so important, I think.*

When you read your own series of stories, it may lead to a feeling of self-verification and coherence, because people across your network know and value your traits. Sure, your strengths may have a shadow side, but it's more motivating and energizing to focus on the positive contributions you make.

The feeling of psychological coherence can be particularly strong when the same signature strengths emerge across *different stages of life*. For example, this is what forty-five-year-old Jacob, a consulting firm partner from New York City, said when he recognized that the stories from his childhood to the stories from his present life almost all reflected his empathy as a strength:

> *Those traits demonstrated from a young age, you know, through my career at forty-plus years old, were pretty consistent. So those capabilities developed very young in my life, and they carried through.*

But some people learn from their highlight reel that the opposite is true. They find there are signature strengths that they demonstrated earlier in life, and then sort of "let go" as their careers took hold and unfolded. Remember, that's exactly what happened with Ben, who found that he was not drawing on his curiosity at work. As Ben put it:

> *It was surprising for me how something which I was really at my best as a child, a teenager, was not really visible*

in my professional life. It was surprising that you can become so "mainstream"—so like a lot of other partners or colleagues. It helped me to re-explore this part of my character.

So, while most people find that their highlight reel makes them feel cohesive and affirmed, some people discover there are core elements of themselves that they are not bringing into all areas of their life.

★ *Kick–Start Your Appreciation Jolt* ★

Take ten minutes to write down some of your own personal reactions to how you were perceived in your stories from your community. When you read your highlight reel, did you gain a sense that people know who you really are *across* your social network? Or did you find a lot of inconsistency between the stories from your work colleagues and your family and friends? What themes were strongest across time, since you were a child to now?

Now that you have completed all four exercises, pull these reflections together side by side. Take a moment to look at all the incredible things you've learned so far, and how experiencing your living eulogy has changed some of your thoughts and perceptions. What are some of the positive effects this process has had on you as a whole?

Consider how odd it is that none of this would have happened without the positive method, because of those invisible forces holding us back from our potential. Now, add your responses to your highlight reel folder.

IMPOSTER SYNDROME

In an earlier section, we saw how sometimes our strengths come so naturally to us that we can ignore them. We think they are simple or small actions, and not worthy of notice. We forget that, compared to other people, these strengths stand out and make a big difference. This may be one of the causes of the "imposter syndrome."

Back in 1978, psychologists Pauline Clance and Suzanne Imes described imposter syndrome as a feeling of "phoniness" in people who believe that they are not intelligent, capable, or creative—despite showing lots of high achievement. While people with imposter syndrome are highly motivated to achieve, they also live in fear of being "found out" or exposed as frauds.

For example, when I was growing up my mom was a secretary who worked her way up to office manager over twenty years. My dad was a truck driver. My grandfather and my uncles were all truck drivers. That is what my older brother became too. No one in my family had attended university.

Instead of trucking, one of my early and enduring strengths was a love of learning. I read almost all the time as a child. I went off to Penn State University instead of driving a truck, and somehow by age twenty-one, I wound up at Cornell pursuing a PhD. I was so naïve about academia that when I accepted Cornell's offer I didn't even know it was one of the Ivy League schools. When a friend's father told me it was, I actually argued with him and he made me look it up!

Four years later, when Georgia Tech offered me a job as a management professor, it almost didn't seem possible to me. It felt truly strange to be teaching MBA students who were mostly older, and far more experienced, than me.

In earlier chapters I have described how, by age thirty-five or so, I found myself sleepwalking though my life. I have often wondered if some of this sleepwalking was caused—in part—by not wanting to rock the boat that got me there. Maybe I felt like I didn't really belong in academia, and I had just fooled people into "letting me in"? Maybe I thought that if I just kept my head down, and said what Cornell taught me to say, I could escape notice and continue sneaking by without getting caught?

In other words, maybe I experienced a little bit of imposter syndrome.

The strange thing about imposter syndrome is a pervasive feeling of self-doubt despite overwhelming evidence to the contrary. The feeling is so deep that it can remain hidden to us even as it affects us. It strikes smart, successful people, often following an especially notable accomplishment, like getting a good job, gaining admission to a prestigious university, or earning a big promotion.

Have you ever felt that maybe you were admitted to a school, or given a job, by mistake? Have you ever worried that you might be revealed as a fraud once people "found out" that you didn't belong? Turns out that many people suffer anxiety-inducing thoughts about their competence or qualifications. Many people wonder if they are really as good as the place in life in which they find themselves.

Take Tom Hanks, for example. Hanks has two Academy Awards and has appeared in more than seventy films and TV shows. Can you imagine how accomplished and confident you would feel to be the star of *Splash, Big, Sleepless in Seattle, Philadelphia, Apollo 13, Toy Story, Saving Private Ryan, You've Got Mail, Charlie Wilson's War,* and *Bridge of Spies*?

But Hanks still finds himself doubting his own abilities:

> *No matter who we are, no matter what we've done, there comes a point where you think,* How did I get here? *and* Am I going to be able to continue this? When are they going to discover that I am, in fact, a fraud and take everything away from me? *It's a high-wire act that we all walk.*

Hanks is far from being alone. Imagine how good it would feel to cement a writing career with three Grammys. Now, throw in being nominated for both a Pulitzer Prize *and* a Tony Award. This was all on the resume of author and poet Maya Angelou. But she still questioned her abilities and talents. As she put it, "I have written eleven books, but each time I think, 'Uh oh, they're going to find out now. I've run a game on everybody, and they're going to find me out.'" Tina Fey, a self-described imposter, deals with her feelings by remembering that "everyone else is an impostor, too."

There seem to be three main causes for the imposter syndrome, all of which may be alleviated by your highlight reel.

First, remember how a fish doesn't know it's wet? The imposter syndrome springs, in part, from the fact that when we have a strength that feels natural to us, we tend to discount its value. The result is that we hesitate to believe that what feels natural to us—maybe even *easy* for us—can offer much value to the world.

Second, trying unfamiliar behaviors always feels uncomfortable at first. When we begin to take on a new role, or activity, it can make us feel fake. According to my colleague Herminia Ibarra at London Business School, an expert on how we change ourselves and take on fresh identities and roles, this is because new behaviors usually do not feel natural, at first. According to Ibarra, unfamiliar behaviors make us feel a little odd, and we often interpret unfamiliarity as "superficial" or "inauthentic." The result is that experimenting with new behaviors can make us feel like a fraud. When we feel this way, it can push us back from trying and learning from novel experiences.

Third, the imposter syndrome emerges from those social norms around pride and humility that we discussed in chapter 4. Excessive pride is bad for society, it is true, and groups work better when members have humility. Taken too far, however, humility holds us back from playing to our strengths, pursuing our potential, and giving the most of ourselves.

The result? Once we have achieved a bit of success, in our careers in particular, maybe we start to wonder if we are good enough to strive for even bigger successes and accomplishments. Maybe we start to think—even subconsciously—that if we just stay in our lane, and don't go out on a limb, people will continue to overlook us rather than exposing us as frauds. This is a sort of "hunker down" mentality, where we just keep doing the same thing that worked for us in the first place. And the problem with this mindset is that it becomes too scary for us to try something new, and so we stop striving to make a bigger impact. So we stop growing and learning. We settle in, and switch to autopilot mode, instead of finding ways to leverage our best selves and pursue our potential.

That's what I think I did in my thirties. My life fell into a rut of routine and playing it safe. And while imposter syndrome held me back from growing, reading my own highlight reel became a major turning point for me.

For many people, feelings of imposter moments are transient. They may kick in after starting a new job or entering an environment in which our minority status is obvious. For some, however, imposter feelings are more pervasive and hinder performance. Women and minorities often may be hit the hardest, because as psychology professor Brad Johnson and sociology professor David Smith put it in their *Harvard Business Review* article, "Hierarchical and masculine cultures can contribute to imposter distress."

Many talented and skilled first-generation college students, and women in STEM fields (science, technology, engineering, and mathematics) sometimes feel they don't belong because they tend to be among a sea of peers whose parents attended college or a minority in a male-dominated program. They can then start to feel like impostors, which results in a self-fulfilling prophecy if they waste energy on worrying rather than bringing their best to the environment. Even though they have the ability to succeed in these programs, their lingering anxiety, negative self-talk, and the background static of believing they are at threat is a negative force in their lives. As we saw in chapter 1, this anxiety can sap our energy and doesn't let us access the creativity and problem-solving skills that we possess.

The imposter syndrome also can become a long-term problem for some people because it implies a "fixed mindset"—meaning that we believe others "have it" and that we "don't have it." This mind-set leads us to believe we will never be able to attain "it," whatever *it* might be, no matter how much harder we strive. The result is that we keep our heads down, try to not mess up, and try to "wait out life" instead of searching for the best way to make our greatest impact. Change and learning involve experimenting. And that doesn't feel safe to do when we are too afraid to take risks or make mistakes because we feel like we just got lucky in the first place to be where we are.

When we see the hard evidence of how capable we are through our highlight reel, we realize that we have the ability to transform and improve—which can completely shift our mindset from fixed to one of growth.

Highlight reels can help with imposter syndrome by revealing the positive impact we make on other people. They allow us to value our strengths appropriately, as the unique value we bring to the world.

For example, Arjun, a student at the University of Michigan, realized how the self-validating stories from his network helped push back his feelings that his accomplishments "happen just by chance." Throughout his life, Arjun said he always got a "feedback sandwich"—which meant that even when people gave him positive insights about himself, they usually positioned one of his limitations between the positive information. This always left him focusing on the negative and disregarding his positive traits.

The highlight reel experience was different for Arjun, because it finally allowed him to focus on his strengths and on how to keep them going, effectively doubling down on what he did best instead of worrying about what he could improve. As he said, "I think that this feedback definitely deflates the imposter syndrome. This actually validates your behavior or your actions, and it gives you confidence."

Antônia experienced imposter syndrome when she was promoted to managing director of her consulting firm. She said, "I don't know, at some point I was feeling 'I'm a fraud.'" Antônia was panicking because she wondered if she had just been a fake, and now was finally being "found out." Creating her highlight reel helped put things into perspective and let her deal with this anxiety head-on:

> *The letters came at such a pivotal moment in my life. It was better than any conversation I think I could have, or any therapy that I could have. I was kind of sad that I had been suffering for a long time. And that I had been hurting myself, being so hard on myself. Saying, "I'm not good, I'm not good. My God, what happened, Antônia, what happened to you? You're not good, you're like an imposter."*

The highlight reel was important for Antônia because these negative feelings and the negative self-talk around her work were making her less effective at her job. They also were spilling over and deteriorating her nonwork attitudes and behaviors:

> *We tend to see the defects, the things we are not doing well, and the things we have to improve. You know: "I'm fat," "My hair is not good," "I'm not doing my job well," "My house is not clean enough," and whatever. And because of that we—not consciously—but we punish ourselves. We say, "I don't deserve this." And then, you don't do what you like in life because you feel you don't deserve it.*

Antônia's insight is really powerful, and sad, for me. First, how can we be so successful in life and yet still be so harsh in evaluating ourselves?

Across her life, Antônia was an achiever. From her humble background, she earned an MBA from a top university and then worked her way up to managing director. She earns in the top 1% of all humans, and she helps people in her job each day. And yet she questioned herself. She doubted her value. She felt like an imposter who was going to be "found out."

That feeling of being threatened doesn't just eat into brain processing that could be used more productively. It also diminishes quality of life.

Antônia's story is also profound because it shows how our harsh self-evaluations can make us punish ourselves. We hold ourselves back from what energizes us in life. We diminish our life experience and create a downward spiral.

And finally, this insight is important because it reminds us why highlight reels can help. By showing us the ways that we are valued by people we care about, highlight reels affirm us. They help us remove some of the useless mental clutter and break the downward spiral of self-deprecating or overly critical thoughts. Many of us are harder on ourselves than we are on other people, always thinking we should be better. Our highlight reels can help us remember that we are okay human beings. They show us that we belong and are valued. We still want to improve, but we see we should be kinder to ourselves on the way.

By revealing how you make a positive difference in other people's lives, your highlight reel may allow you to become more caring toward yourself, even as you strive to become your best possible self.

DO NO HARM

Most of what people experience with their highlight reels is positive, and the science also shows many positive outcomes. However, I'd like to spend a little time talking about two types of negative experiences that I have learned about highlight reels:

1) Why didn't you say even nicer things about me? Did anyone disappoint you with what they wrote—or didn't write—about you? This is important, because by definition you reached out to some of the most significant people in the world to you. And it is likely that some people in your network were much more giving of their time, or more giving of their vulnerability and emotions.

When I read my report, for example, some people wrote several paragraphs and gave lots of good details that helped me relive and savor the memories. These stories were powerful and emotional for me to read. Other people just wrote a sentence or two, which really paled by comparison. Instead of writing "to me" about specific memories, their short sentences felt more like a performance review. At the time, I wished they instead gave me the deeper perspective that other people in my network did.

It also is possible when you read your highlights from certain people that you were surprised they did not write about specific memories. This came up in several of my interviews with people who created highlight reels. Sometimes we are just *sure* that a person will write about that one special moment, but then are disappointed because the person did not mention that important story. Maybe a person did not write about some of your traits that you were *sure* add the most value (and should be appreciated by them, dammit!).

The simple reality is we can't control the stories our community gives us and there are times people do not write the stories you hoped for.

In a class I was teaching at London Business School, one forty-five-year-old woman by the name of June told me that her mother wrote three memories about her, all from when she was a child. June asked the other seventy-five people in our class, angrily, "I mean, have I not done ANYTHING in the last thirty years that she might have found impressive?!"

It was a strangely charged moment, because I think much of the class could relate to a time when someone they cared about did not see them the same way they saw themselves. This can be frustrating and painful sometimes. But in cases like these, we have to remember that these people are not intentionally trying to hurt us; they want us to do well and to be happy. And perhaps, we have to help them get to know us better, the way we see ourselves.

Despite prompting them, some people also may not even respond with stories, just a list of adjectives about you that don't form any sort of beginning, middle, or end. The words just dangle there.

And some people you ask for stories may not respond at all, or may decline to offer any feedback. This happened to Louise from Paris, who confided the following:

> My husband refused to complete it, which I was extremely sad about. I know my husband well enough that I was not surprised. So I would say "hurt" is not maybe the right word as much as "disappointed." But I moved on.

Naturally, it would be possible to think less of the people who don't write about the things you expected, or do not respond at all, especially after you took the time to provide them with good memories. It would be easy to let a lackluster response scar your relationship with someone.

That's what I am worried about. As I have been urging you to reach out with the positive method, I worry that some of these outcomes could possibly harm a relationship, if you are not mindful. What I'd like us to consider instead is generosity in taking from people what they are able to give.

Each person in your network is in a different place right now. Some people have the time, energy, and mindset to reflect and write. Others do not. We talked about how strange the positive method can feel, and some people just may not know how to handle it. Some people are better writers than other people, and it might come easier to them (a signature strength!). Some people are closer to the science of positive psychology than other people and are more practiced with giving gratitude. Remember, you are strengthening all these relationships from different starting points.

In the end, different people are at different stages of their journey through life. Whatever they write, or don't write, does not have to make them bad people. It does not have to imply a bad relationship.

Practice letting go of any disappointment that you may feel. Treat the process of creating your highlight reel as an experiment and generously receive what people are able to offer.

2) My highlight reel didn't do enough. Most people experience the appreciation jolt of the highlight reel if they save up the stories to read all at once and read them in the right environment. They get a feel-good hit of dopamine. They cry when reading their report, and they are touched emotionally. But a year later, they realize their emotions and actions have drifted back to their personal average.

If you want to improve your life and become your own version of exceptional, it is not enough to *know* your strengths. You have to find new ways to *use* your strengths.

Let me tell you about some research conducted by Martin Seligman. One year, whenever people visited Seligman's website, he recruited them to join a study. He randomly put the 577 men and women who signed up into different groups. He told one group to take that online survey of character strengths that I shared with you in chapter 7, which as you know gives validated feedback.

Another group was told to take the same online survey, but also was told to use one of their top strengths *in a new way* every day for one week. For example, if somebody's signature strength was curiosity, they might take on a new task at work that uses that strength or join a class about a topic that was new to them. If their top strength was kindness, they might take on a volunteer role.

Then, Seligman tracked everyone for six months and compared them to a control group that lived their normal lives and was not told to try anything new. Everyone in the study reported their life fulfillment and their depressive symptoms. Fulfillment was measured by how often people experienced pleasure, lost themselves in engaging activities, and the like. Depressive symptoms include feeling lonely and depressed, restless sleep, and trouble getting going in the morning.

Here is what the results showed: For people who took the survey and became more *familiar* with their signature strengths, they felt better than the control group in the short run. They were more fulfilled for a few weeks. But then the effect faded, and there was no difference between them and the control group six months later.

But get this: The group that used their signature strengths in a new way became happier, and less depressed, in the long run. I don't mean that these people became happier for a week or two. People who used their signature strengths in a new way were still doing better than the control group six months later, when the study ended.

Myriam Mongrain and Tracy Anselmo-Matthews, professors of psychology at York University, then replicated Seligman's findings with a large Canadian sample. They confirmed that people became statistically happier in life when they started using their signature strengths in new ways to create new habits.

These results suggest it is not enough to *know* your strengths; you also need to *stretch* into your strengths with new behaviors. This is exactly what you will learn to do in this next and final step of the positive method. You will learn how to create new habits, expand your strengths, and, most importantly, craft your life around what you do best.

STEP 3

CHAPTER 9

Stretching into Our Strengths

M any of us are capable of making a much bigger impact in our lives than we are currently making. We're not being our own version of exceptional as often as we could. Here is how William James, the first educator to offer a psychology course in the United States, said it: "Compared with what we ought to be, we are only half awake. Our fires are damped, our drafts are checked. We are making use of only a small part of our possible mental resources."

This book is all about waking up to your potential. So far, you have learned how you can improve the story you tell about yourself. Then you built a highlight reel that helped you pinpoint your signature strengths. Hopefully, you are already feeling the positive momentum from this process. Hopefully, you also felt a jolt of appreciation that helped you question some of your assumptions about life and put into perspective what you are truly capable of.

You've made a lot of progress to get this far! You should feel good about that. But in order to actually transform your life, you need to find a way to *trigger your exceptionality regularly.* Your highlight reel showed you some big and small moments throughout your life where you exercised your signature strengths; I bet you want to see yourself tapping into moments like those more often. To do this, you need to make lasting changes to your behaviors. *To become exceptional, you need to make a daily habit of using your signature strengths.*

Welcome to step 3. Over the next few chapters, this is exactly what you will learn to do. You'll discover how to chronically access what makes you exceptional. This begins with understanding how to create lasting change and how we make new habits stick.

CHANGE IS EASY

Luckily, change is easy. It's just as easy as writing your name.

With your other hand, that is.

Try it: Write your name down in the margin of this book or a piece of paper. But don't use the hand that you normally use; use the other hand. What feelings are you experiencing as you write? Does it feel uncomfortable? Unnatural? Perhaps you feel a bit childish?

Did you find that you wrote your name faster or slower with your other hand? Does this version of your name look better or worse?

This writing exercise shows you how change is not just a cognition. We often think of change as something that shifts in the mind, and while, of course, that is part of it, change is not something you only think about. Change is physical. From smaller changes (like learning to use a new phone) to bigger changes (like starting a new job), it involves moving your hands, arms, legs, and mouth in new ways.

Why do you think it felt uncomfortable and awkward to write with your other hand? After all, you're using the same pen or pencil. You're writing the same name and using the same letters you've used your whole life. Both your hands have the same bone structure, muscles, and nerves. So why these awkward feelings? Why is it taking longer? Why does it not look as smooth?

The answer is practice.

In life, everything is hard before it gets easy. Nobody learns how to walk without falling, learning, and practicing. Writing your name, giving a speech, driving a car—none of these things is easy the first time. But then after we practice fifty times, and then five hundred times, it becomes second nature. Repetition makes it feel natural. It becomes hard to remember that it was ever hard. Consistent practice is how you build a new habit.

A few years ago, my older daughter Daisy and I started bouldering, where you climb up walls of plastic "rocks" without a harness or ropes. It's exhilarating and a little scary as you get higher up. It's a lot like the movie *Free Solo*—except there are two of us, and we only climb twelve-foot walls, and there are soft mats under us.

Bouldering demands biceps and strong grip, so my daughter and I installed a pull-up bar in the doorway to her room. The first time she tried to do a pull-up, her face was straining but her body wasn't moving.

She was persistent, trying it once or twice each day. Within a month she could pull herself up three inches. We tracked her progress with pencil marks along the doorframe that measured how high her feet went. After three months she could pull herself up a foot off the ground. After six months she completed her first pull-up. What changed was *physical*: When she started, the muscle simply was not there. But each attempt demanded more from her biceps, and the muscle adapted. It became stronger.

Our brains work like muscles. They physically change and strengthen with practice. For example, despite the prevalence of GPS, London taxi drivers still have to take "the knowledge," a series of tests that includes memorizing the map of the city in order to be licensed. Think of it as having an atlas of London implanted into your brain. To do this, they must learn huge quantities of information about London's twenty-five thousand streets and twenty thousand landmarks. It takes two to four years! And when they undergo this learning, their actual brain changes. Specifically, the physical part of the brain that deals with spatial information, the hippocampal area, gets larger (this does not happen for bus drivers, because bus drivers follow similar daily routes and do not learn all that information).

Pretty cool, right? Just like my daughter's bicep got bigger as it adapted, the actual biology of the brain changes as taxi drivers strengthen their nodes and neural connections.

The ability of our minds to alter and strengthen is called "neuroplasticity"—and it is at the very heart of human behavior. The magic here is that we can cause our neurons to *selectively strengthen* certain connections with one another. Remember from chapter 2: The more often we recall a memory, the stronger its neural network becomes. Through consistent recall, the memory becomes "encoded" in a part of the brain called the cortex, the place in charge of long-term storage.

I tell you all this because it is key to accessing your signature strengths more often. You can think of this as the *biology* of becoming exceptional.

When you first try a new behavior—like writing with your other hand—the neurons and the linkages are weak and underdeveloped. That's why it's slow going. It feels unnatural, as if we were "using" our hand like a puppet. We have to carefully watch ourselves writing each letter, constantly instructing our hand as we observe what is working and what is not working. The process is laborious and, well, *manual*. It demands our focus. (You can almost hear yourself talking to yourself: "Pull the pen down, down, down, okay STOP. Now, go to the right.") The result looks amateur.

But what happens if you practice this one thousand times? If you keep sending the demand to write with that hand, the neurons and the linkages develop around your demands. Instead of a small path for information to flow, the linkages become a superhighway. Information zooms quickly and easily. Eventually, you don't even have to think about it anymore. This is called *automaticity*. Your hand does the behavior naturally without even looking. Your brain is freed up to work on other things, and it feels comfortable and natural.

As you can see, it's going to take consistent practice of stretching your signature strengths in new ways to make the stretching into a habit. Even if you are only practicing your strengths a little each day, the key is to continue to use them regularly. This is how you make your possible impact on other people and the world. You will learn more about how to incorporate your strengths into your life in big and small ways in the next chapter.

POWERING THROUGH THE UNCOMFORTABLE

As we have made our way through the book together, we've seen that a lot of society's commonly held assumptions are simply wrong.

- Sharing gratitude for others' contributions doesn't make relationships awkward; instead, it makes relationships stronger.

- Creating a highlight reel is not selfish; instead, it illuminates your signature strengths, which helps you improve the lives of others.

- Learning about your most exceptional qualities doesn't make you arrogant and complacent; instead, it makes you humble and energized to work harder.

- Ignoring our transience doesn't solve problems; instead, it creates problems like putting our gifts on hold.

By now, you can probably see how the two hidden forces—the eulogy delay and transience aversion—result in these false assumptions and hold us all back from reaching our real potential. So, in this chapter, we are overturning one more incorrect assumption:

Playing to your strengths doesn't mean coasting; instead, it means living up to your potential and working harder to shine your light in bigger and brighter ways.

When you live your life making the best use of your strengths, it creates a sense of relief—but this isn't because it's easy. The relief comes from no longer trying to be anyone but yourself. When you are doing what you love and what you are good at, you experience relief because you are living authentically, true to what you were made to do.

In this way, using your gifts creates less friction in your life, because you are acting according to your values and finding more fulfillment. But it doesn't always mean smooth sailing. It takes a lot of courage to make the changes necessary to live authentically, and it takes courage to choose to do things in *your own way*. As e. e. cummings put it, "To be nobody but yourself in a world which is doing its best, night and day, to make you everybody else, means to fight the hardest battle which any human being can fight."

Your combination of signature strengths, values, and dreams are unique to you. This is how they make you exceptional.

And this is why many people find that reading their highlight reels creates a weight of responsibility. Because activating what makes you exceptional means investing more of yourself than perhaps you are used to, and doing things differently than others might be used to. Stretching into your strengths—embracing them in new settings and activities—requires you to leave your comfort zone. When you read your highlight reel, you will likely be inspired to rise to this exceptional version of yourself, not just once, but in a lifelong way. This is exactly how Coma Dave felt:

> *Getting to read my own eulogies finally gave me the gravitas I always felt I deserved, but with that gravitas came an unexpected weight. I felt I had to live up to all of the positive things everyone said about me . . . I couldn't just do nothing and expect eulogy-level attention to roll in constantly.*

Once you see your potential more clearly, it becomes almost impossible to ignore. You start to see how not using a gift is letting it go to waste. In order to live up to your own version of exceptional, you will have to be bold, playing to your strengths in order to make potential into reality. Trust me, you will be so grateful to have powered through the discomfort this can create, because it will change the way you live.

Less than a year after I joined London Business School as a professor, I was asked to take on the role of department chair. I had never held this position before. And it is a funny role because most professors don't consider the department chair their "boss"—in fact, most professors don't think that they have a boss. Autonomy and freedom are the perks of the job that draw people to academia in the first place.

Anyway, when I took on the department chair role, I was filling the capable shoes of a professor who had helped grow the department and the school into a world-class institution. He had a very strong sense of what he wanted to accomplish and how it should be done. To this day, one of his signature strengths is deep knowledge and understanding of networks. He is politically savvy, and he knows how to get things done. He knows who holds the formal and informal power over decisions and resources. He had spent a decade fostering strong relationships with influential people in the school.

When I took on the new role, I was new to the scene at London Business School. I knew almost nothing about the social and political network. Also, anyone who knows me knows I am not politically savvy. And leading with absolute certainty is the opposite of my approach to life and work. I subscribe to "humble leadership," which starts with asking the people you serve, "How can I help you do your work?"

Unfortunately for me, the team I was leading expected things to run the same way as it had in the past. However, when I tried to "work on my limitations" in order to use the same leadership approach, I was very ineffective. I felt demoralized. You kind of become a living joke if you teach leadership but you can't lead. I can remember trying to run meetings like the previous chairperson did, watching as chaos erupted when we talked about issues that had not already been resolved in advance. I was not succeeding in my new role.

Based on what I learned from my highlight reel, I gathered together the confidence to try playing to my signature strengths, rather than trying to copy the style of the former leader. A recurring theme throughout my highlight reel was expressing myself in a way that opens other people up. For example, one person wrote the following:

> *Dan makes others feel comfortable in his company and therefore allows others to express themselves without being overly conscious. In the workplace this means co-workers feel at ease expressing their opinions, concerns, and suggestions.*

This theme emerged again and again in my highlight reel, across friends, family, and former work colleagues. So, I started working harder to display this strength in the role of department chair. Of course, this did not solve everything right away. I know I did not get everything right. But I found myself much more energized trying to accomplish tasks using my own style and approach. Conversations and meetings seemed to go a lot better, and over the next two years we made some progress as a group. And I soon received feedback from colleagues that they noticed and appreciated me using this trait.

But what happens if I had started with the assumption that improvement only comes from fixing my weaknesses? Then "playing to my strengths" would feel like cheating. For many people, building highlight reels and emphasizing strengths just seems too "positive" to create real results—even if the science tells us otherwise. But if we are going to strive for something, shouldn't we put our time and energy into areas where we shine, rather than working twice as hard futilely trying to fix our limitations?

Even when it's not easy, it feels good to stretch into our strengths. It can create positive momentum and an upward spiral. We end up feeling more motivated and energized when we feel authentic and able to spend our time exercising our unique gifts.

ADOPT A GROWTH MINDSET TO BUILD ON STRENGTHS

As we have established, when it comes to change, it first gets uncomfortable before it starts to feel natural. It is impossible to avoid this struggle when we are trying to improve ourselves. But it *is* possible to change the way you *interpret* the discomfort. And the way you interpret it makes all the difference, according to Carol Dweck, professor of psychology at Stanford University and the author of *Mindset.*

One way you can interpret that feeling of struggle is as "mistakes." I mean, look at how your name looks in the margin when you wrote it with your other hand. It looks like a mess. And it took longer to write than usual. And it felt awkward. You could do it a lot more efficiently if you just used your regular hand, right? If you interpret the discomfort of learning as "messing up," it's called an *achievement mindset.* People who hold an *achievement mindset* think the most important thing is getting it right, proving their competence, and succeeding in what they already know how to do well.

Decades of solid scientific evidence shows us that an *achievement mindset* makes us more likely to revert to our old habits when new behaviors become uncomfortable. This makes sense: If you interpret learning as failure, then you stop learning and just do what has worked in the past. After all, it goes faster, looks better, and feels more comfortable. We stick with known behaviors to avoid embarrassment and the risk of failure. Thus, *an achievement mindset is playing not to lose.*

Unfortunately, when we revert to the old habits, then we don't challenge ourselves. We don't build the neurons that let the brain do its plasticity thing, the physical changes we learned about with the London taxi drivers' brains. When we don't practice a new behavior, we never make the new behavior our own. And therefore, it never becomes a new habit.

From chapter 8, you are already familiar with the work of my London Business School colleague Herminia Ibarra. Ibarra warns us about what she calls the *authenticity trap*. When you begin to experiment with new activities, even when you play to your strengths, you feel awkward until you practice them enough to make them your own. Ibarra's research suggests that instead of becoming imprisoned by habit, you need to be playful with practice. When you start trying out new behaviors in the next chapter, stay curious and playful instead of thinking it will go perfectly the first time. It usually won't.

So, it may sound a little crazy, but if you are trying to improve your life, an *achievement mindset* won't work. Luckily, there is a better way. You can interpret the awkwardness as evidence that you are learning and getting stronger. This is called a *growth mindset*. Decades of scientific evidence make it clear that when we adopt a *growth mindset*, we are more likely to persevere. Because when we interpret our struggle with learning as practice, we're more likely to stick with it and get our brains to internalize the new habits. Building new mental muscle this way is how you develop true confidence in a new behavior and take full advantage of your strengths.

A *growth mindset* helps you "go for the gold" while an *achievement mindset* tells you to "play it safe." This is where the psychology of mindset meets up with the biology of the brain. What I mean is that our physical brains will build new neural connections to align with the demands we give it, but this might not feel comfortable at first. As you practice your strengths, try to take on a *growth mindset* and see adaptation as progress, not failure.

CREATE A VISION OF YOUR BEST FUTURE SELF

To go for your gold and create the improvements you want to make in life, you need a vision of how life will look when you get there as the person you most want to be. You'll learn about and create a vision for your future here in this section. Then, in the next section, you'll see how you can train your brain to adapt and help you achieve it.

According to Hazel Markus, a Michigan professor and one of the leading authorities on self-research, we gain resilience in the face of temporary challenges by recalling memories of past successes (your highlight reel) and by envisioning our best future selves. In a study conducted by Markus and Ann Ruvolo from Notre Dame, they told one group of people to visualize themselves being successful in the future due to their own hard work:

> *Imagine yourself in the future. Everything has gone as well as it possibly could have. You have worked hard and succeeded in achieving your goals. What are you imagining? What do you see yourself doing? What kind of environment are you in? What type of people are around you? Describe how you feel in your imagined scene. In this imagined scene, what do you do on a typical day?*

Ruvolo and Markus told a second group to imagine themselves being unsuccessful in the future, *despite* their hard work ("You have worked very hard but have failed to achieve your goals"). Then they were asked to write about the same questions as the first group. Meanwhile, the researchers also gave a third control group an article about the sun and stars to read and a small bag of candy to induce a positive mood. All of the participants then performed two tasks, one demanding effort and another involving persistence. Which group of participants do you think did better?

Participants who imagined themselves experiencing success performed significantly better on both types of tasks. Ruvolo and Markus's research showed that those who imagined working very hard to achieve their own success had more positive working self-concepts, which likely gave them the confidence and motivation to power through the tasks they were given.

Ruvolo and Markus's study showed how envisioning our best future self can improve the way we perform, but some related research also shows it can improve our health. In one investigation, Laura King, a psychology professor at the University of Missouri, asked four groups of undergraduates to write about one of four topics for twenty minutes each day, for four consecutive days.

One group of participants was assigned to write about their best possible future self using the same approach as Ruvolo and Markus used (e.g., "Think about your life in the future. Imagine that everything has gone as well as it possibly could"). Another group of individuals was assigned to write in detail about a traumatic life event, while a third group of students was asked to spend two writing sessions on each of these topics. A final group served as a control—they were asked to write about their plans for the day in detail.

In a survey three weeks later, King found that students who wrote about their best future selves experienced an increase in life satisfaction that was higher than the other groups. This is a nice result, but perhaps not too surprising. Perhaps more amazing were the health results. The students who wrote about their best future selves were statistically less likely to get sick and visit the university health center in the five months following the writing exercises.

Wow. The long-term effects of this writing exercise are really incredible. And remember that it did not take people very long to do. We're talking about twenty minutes a day for four days to experience more fulfillment and better health. Now, it's time to try King's experiment for yourself.

★ *Envision Your Best Future Self* ★

Dedicate twenty minutes each day for the next four days to your own Best Future Self exercise, by writing a "letter from the future" to yourself.

Here is what you do: Imagine yourself in the future, and then describe to yourself what it will be like when you get there. "Hey me," you say in your writing. "This is how life looks and feels when I am fully using my strengths and doing what I do best."

I did this exact same exercise myself ten years ago, when I first moved to London right after I wrapped up my chemo. I wrote, and wrote, and then I wrote some more about how I thought my future could be if I was at my best. After several sessions of writing, I found that I was thinking about six dimensions of life, which might be helpful to consider as you complete this exercise:

- **Socially**, who will I be around?
- **Psychologically**, what will I feel like? What sort of mindset will I have?
- **Professionally**, what activities will I be involved with? What will I be achieving?
- **Recreationally**, what activities will help regenerate me? What will I be doing for fun?
- **Educationally**, how will I be learning and improving?
- **Physically**, how active will I be, and with what activities?

This was a lot for me to work through. And that's one of the reasons why you need to put in the time across four days, and not try to do it all at once. It actually takes a while to let your mind explore each dimension of your life.

This is a big commitment, I know. The temptation will be to not *actually* do this exercise, and just read on. This would be like reading about working out instead of going to the gym. It won't actually make you any stronger. Your best self is right there, just waiting to be unleashed! And taking the steps to visualize that possible self will help motivate you and push you to pursue that future.

So, find a time and a place where you can contemplate and reflect in peace, without being interrupted. Maybe, for you, this is in the morning instead of reading the paper for a week. For me, it was before bed, when everyone else in the house was asleep. You could use the six categories that I developed, or make up your own, or you could write more holistically.

When you have finished, put your work in your highlight reel folder.

To help me write this chapter I went back and read my own Best Future Self exercise, which I had completed almost ten years ago. It felt like opening a time capsule, and it was a really interesting and powerful experience. I was surprised and really happy to see what I had written at the end of it:

Writing this out, I can see now that—at least at work—this is my purpose: to wake people up to the fact that you have just one life to live. Let's not choke on that one chance to be the best selves we can be, the easiest and hardest thing to do in the world. It strikes me that rather than doing what we really want to be doing with our time, many of us find that we are trying not to make waves; we're trying to sneak through life without incident. We're trying not to lose what we have.

I didn't know it until now, but it looks like this book actually started ten years ago!

After you have completed your Best Future Self exercise, be sure to hold on to it. But don't wait ten years to look at it like I did—get it back out and read it once a year, maybe on your birthday or maybe on New Year's. It's a great way to sharpen your ideals and goals and look at how your behaviors are aligning with your best possible future. It's a great way to check in with yourself. You may even consider doing the exercise again if you feel your goals for your future have changed.

TRAINING YOUR MIND FOR CHANGE

Let me introduce you to a study by Lien Pham and Shelley Taylor at UCLA. They observed undergraduates as they prepared for their psychology midterm exams. They gave all the participants a daily calendar and asked them to indicate the days and hours that they planned to study for the exam, and where and how they planned to study.

Some of the participants were then instructed to *mentally simulate* themselves studying: "Visualize yourself studying for the midterm in such a way that would lead you to obtain a high grade on the midterm. As of today and for the remaining days before the midterm, imagine how you would study to get a high grade on your psychology midterm. It is very important that you see yourself actually studying and have that picture in your mind."

Other participants were instructed to visualize themselves having achieved a very high score: "Visualize yourself getting a high grade on your psychology midterm and imagine how you would feel. It is very important that you see yourself actually getting a high grade on the psychology midterm and have that picture in your mind."

A final group was the control group. They simply recorded the hours they studied each day for the exam.

Based on what you've learned so far, what do you think the results were? You guessed it: Students who simulated step by step *how* they would study scored significantly better on the test than the other two groups. These students were able to develop clear and detailed plans about exactly how and when they would study, which reduced their anxiety and made them more confident, putting them in a better emotional state to take the exam. This visualization also made them more likely to follow through with their plans: They studied more hours and were able to manage their anxiety better.

But get this: Students who envisioned getting a good grade performed worst of all! They scored even lower than the control group. They also studied *five hours less*, on average. It's almost like dreaming about succeeding made them think they were off the hook from actually working hard to get there.

This is similar to research by Gabriele Oettingen and Thomas Wadden, professors at UPenn, who found that people's positive fantasies diminished success in a weight loss program, with effects that lasted a full year afterward. By fantasizing about the outcome and not imaging the behavioral steps to get there, participants simulated the emotions of already accomplishing their goal, which decreased their feelings of motivations and drive.

Fantasizing about outcomes, like good grades or weight loss, doesn't help unless you make specific behavioral changes. This would be the equivalent of you just thinking you will be happy ten years from now in your Best Future Self exercise. But you did not just think about "being fulfilled"—instead, you carefully visualized what projects and activities you would be doing that would help you create fulfillment.

Having a detailed vision of how to accomplish our goals is necessary because it allows us to mentally prepare for the task ahead, and it builds confidence to know we have a plan. In the same way that the students from Pham and Taylor's study mentally simulated their successful studying, we need to envision ourselves acting out our signature strengths with new activities. We need to train our brains to picture step by step how our strengths will be incorporated into our daily routines, resulting in a better reality.

HOW LONG DOES IT TAKE TO CREATE A HABIT?

How long must we practice and play with new behaviors before they start to become comfortable habits? According to Professor Phillippa Lally and her colleagues from University College London, it can take about two months with steady practice. These researchers studied people who were interested in forming a healthy new habit—such as eating a piece of fruit with lunch or doing a fifteen-minute run each day. After each day, for twelve weeks, participants reported whether they tried the new behavior that day. Then, they reported how "natural" and "automatic" their new behavior felt.

On average, participants reached a plateau in automaticity after sixty-six days. In other words, in about two months the new behavior had become relatively natural—it had become a habit. Of course, there were differences depending on what new habit people were working on. Drinking a daily glass of water became automatic quickly. Doing fifty sit-ups before breakfast required a longer time and more dedication. The largest gains occurred in the first few weeks of practice, when the new behavior likely felt the most difficult to the participants.

In the next chapter, you'll use your signature strengths to develop a plan of behavioral experiments to help move you toward your vision of your best future. We'll follow the same approach that Lally and her colleagues used, so that you can track yourself using your strengths to form new habits.

The focused changes of these behavioral experiments add up; they are what make it possible to transform your life.

CHAPTER 10

Life Crafting

"Do the best you can until you know better.
When you know better, do better."

—MAYA ANGELOU

s your life overflowing with responsibilities and tasks? Even when something is good for us, it can often feel impossible to add *another* activity or a new habit to our already hectic schedules. For many of us, even after we carve out the time, we may find ourselves asking, "How am I also supposed to find the reserve of energy to charge into this new activity in a meaningful way?"

The truth is, there may never be enough time in our day-to-day lives to accomplish everything we want. But because of the transient nature of life, we simply do not have the luxury of waiting until a new habit fits perfectly into our agenda. And if we wait to use our gifts until the time is "just right," we may never experience that version of our best future self we created in chapter 9. This is why we want to learn how to prioritize the things in our lives that bring forward our strengths.

When you reposition your life to gravitate around your best qualities and what inspires you, you are doing what is called *life crafting*. In this chapter you'll learn how to make a habit of using your signature strengths more often and how to craft a life that helps activate your own version of exceptional.

Picture this as more of a marathon than a sprint. Life crafting doesn't mean changing everything at once. It starts with introducing just one new behavior or strength into your life at a time. Once that behavior becomes a habit, you can then start practicing a new one.

What about your energy levels? Maybe you had just enough energy this week to get through your to-do list. Maybe all you want to do after a long day is order a pizza and watch your favorite TV show. But remember the upward spirals? Small positive changes can lead to large outcomes because they build your energy levels and resilience. It sounds backwards, because it kind of is counterintuitive, but investing energy in the activities that help you shine will give you more energy.

Remember Antônia from São Paulo, Brazil, who watched her dad studying late into the night and dreamed of college in the United States? As a partner in a consulting firm and an extremely hard worker, it was not easy for Antônia to make space in her demanding schedule. For many, many years, she simply did not budget time for the things that made her thrive.

For example, Antônia always knew that going dancing and interacting with her friends and like-minded people improved her mood and gave her more energy. On top of this, she knew she had a natural talent for dancing. After reading some of the stories her college friends shared in her highlight reel, she felt validated about this strength and decided to enroll in a dance class that met every week. A few months later, she committed to going out dancing every other weekend with friends at her favorite bar:

> Some people ask me, "How can you do that? How come you don't need to sleep?" But I feel so energized, going out with people that I like and talking. And then also meeting new people. And now I have a set of new friends that I found, that also like going out and dancing and talking. It's great, and I feel totally energized.

You may or may not like dancing yourself, but the point here is bigger than dancing. The point is that, to get more meaning and joy out of life, we need to invest time and energy in what makes us flourish.

If we step back and think about Antônia's seemingly small but important investments, it represents a life shift. Antônia had not been allowing herself to enjoy activities like dance before reading her highlight reel. Why? Do you remember, she was punishing herself? She was focusing all her resources on improving her limitations, and trying to meet other people's standards, and therefore felt she didn't deserve to set aside time for what she loved:

> *I felt at some points in my life, "I'm not worthy of having time for myself." And I think it happens to a lot of people. I guess today I'm considering more what I like, not what other people like.*

Think of the potential energy that was being wasted over the years as Antônia ignored her natural exuberance. After investing in her strengths, Antônia became a better friend and a better leader, as her vitality and her sense of fulfillment increased. She told me she felt like she tapped into a well of energy, resulting in more enthusiasm about life.

It takes both courage and commitment to pursue what we want to do with our one unique opportunity to live, rather than what we think other people think we should be doing. And more practically, it takes dedication to push other activities out of the way, each of them squawking like baby birds in the nest, hungry for our time and attention. In order to be our own version of exceptional we can't adhere to everyone else's standards. We have to create our own criteria for what we believe is a well-lived life and focus in on that.

When I went back and read my own Best Future Self exercise, I saw that ten years ago I had written this:

> *I would have a great, fun relationship with Alison. We'd be doing things together that we both liked and thought were interesting, and we'd both still be learning.*

Since that time, one of the new activities that we added to our lives is a fiction course. Alison and I initially met in a literature class, and we both feel joy exploring literature and learning together. However, somehow over the course of our relationship we'd lost our focus on this. Six years ago, we found a literature teacher in our neighborhood who holds classes right in her living room, and we have been exploring great works of fiction together ever since. In the last two years we've read and unpacked *The English Patient* by Michael Ondaatje, *Ulysses* by James Joyce, *The Wasteland* by T. S. Eliot, and many more.

On the one hand, it lights us up to exercise our love of learning with a literature class. Learning new things is a signature strength we both share. We leave the weekly sessions feeling refreshed and stimulated, with greater empathy for each other and people in general. Walking home, the world looks brighter to me. Alison and I feel more connected, and it feels like we are digging into rich soil.

On the other hand, adding the classes to our full lives certainly does not come easy. Scheduling the two-hour sessions into our busy calendars and leaving the kids is the least of the commitment, because we read several chapters to prepare for each session. Making the time for both the reading and the class means pushing other demands and opportunities aside. Making changes to improve our lives requires commitment and real hours of practice. But the intellectual engagement we feel with learning, and with each other, as we walk home buzzing with ideas is worth it.

ADDING NEW ACTIVITIES

Many of the stories in Antônia's highlight reel revealed her exuberant attitude toward life. As we saw, she began to find new and different ways to exercise this signature strength, whether that was a dance class or finding more ways to socialize with friends. This enriched her personal life so much that it spilled over into other areas.

Positive psychology research makes it clear that, to improve our satisfaction with life, we must continue to find new ways to use our strengths. Remember the studies in chapter 9, for example, where some participants were told to use one of their top strengths *in a new way* for one week (e.g., join a class or volunteer)? Six months later, these individuals reported greater life satisfaction and less depression than other participants who only *learned* about their signature strengths but didn't use them in new activities.

As you can imagine, using your strengths in the same way routinely can become repetitive and sometimes can even lead to sleepwalking through life. Finding new ways to do what you do best inspires you to keep growing.

When you stretch out your strengths and deepen them, you have the potential to make a bigger positive impact on your community and the lives of others. Life is fragile—it's best to get started today. Try to learn what influence you are capable of creating, while you still have the time.

In the next section, I'm going to suggest a series of exercises that you can use to stretch into your strengths in new ways. You don't have to do them all or do them in any specific order—I just want to give you options to craft your life around your best self.

★ *Transform Your Strengths into New Actions* ★

It's time to create a practice journal that will help you track and monitor your progress toward becoming exceptional. Whether you have a digital or physical journal, the most important thing is simply to have space to log how and when you are practicing your strengths.

For this exercise, look back at the strengths you identified in chapter 7.

Choose one strength to focus on for now. How might you craft your life more around this strength?

Now, write the one signature strength you'd like to focus on at the top of a blank page in your practice journal. Next, brainstorm and write down ten to fifteen different new ways you could use this strength. You may never pursue some of these options, so don't worry about constraining yourself. You simply want to have lots of ideas that are specific to you and your best qualities. It might be a class that connects with your natural interests—such as the literature class for me or dancing for Antônia.

Here are just a few examples, inspired by Martin Seligman's book *Flourish*, of how you might match your strengths with a new activity:

- If your signature strength is creativity, set aside two hours a few evenings each week to write a screenplay, draw, work on some art, or compose a song. Try anything that exercises and expands your creativity and lets you express yourself.

- If you identify with optimism as a strength, find some activities that let you share your optimism or do something to help others make positive change. For example, as a daily cyclist, you might help a group petition for better bike lanes. Or you might start a blog in which you inspire others to take part in something you care about.

- If your strength is appreciation of beauty, try taking a longer, more beautiful route to work even though it adds twenty minutes to your commute. Set aside an hour in your schedule to go for a walk and study nature. Go to a local museum and spend some time gazing at a favorite painting or exploring a new exhibition.

- Regardless of the particular nature of your strength, volunteering is a way to bring your best self to a new setting. One of the real benefits of volunteering is that you set the terms of your involvement, and you can treat it as a playground for exercising your strengths. The point is that entering a new setting prompts you to use your skills in different ways.

Of the new behaviors you wrote down, now select the one that seems most enticing to you. Take ten minutes to think specifically about how, where, and when you can experiment and practice that behavior. Write down who would be around you, and what is the event and environment that would cue this new behavior?

Next, open a calendar and figure out what date is sixty-six days from today. Write that date down in your practice journal, next to the new activity you are going to try (for example, working on an optimistic blog or volunteering in a way that uses your strengths). During this practice period, try to experiment with this activity as often as possible. Ideally, this practice would be daily, to start to make a habit around using the strength.

Finally, at the end of each day, take ten minutes before bed to write down in your practice journal whether or not you were able to exercise the new behavior. If the answer is "no," reflect and write about why you were not able to practice today and how you will adapt to practice the new behavior tomorrow. If the answer is "yes," describe how the practice went for you. How did it make you feel? Who did it affect, and how? How natural or automatic did the behavior feel?

Across the weeks, especially with daily practice, you'll probably start to notice how the new activity makes you feel unique and energized. You may find that your impact on other people becomes more extraordinary, more often. Or that you are motivated to integrate your strengths into more areas of your day-to-day life, which encourages you to start practicing another of the behaviors you wrote on your earlier list. As new behaviors become good habits, old behaviors and habits will get pushed aside to make room. With every new activity you add, you are one step closer to crafting a life around what you do best, and who you are at your best.

WHO AM I BEING?

In addition to trying out new activities, you can bring forward what makes you exceptional with a broader attitude shift. As you go through your day, check in with yourself and ask, "Who am I being right now?" It can be a very powerful question, because it reminds us that we have a choice to make about who shows up when we walk in a room. As you interact with your partner, with friends, with your colleagues, or with your children, examine which of your selves is salient. Are you activating, and projecting, you at your best?

Remember Gabriela, the consulting firm partner living in Bogotá who learned English from watching TV after her childhood horse-riding injury? She is one of the reasons I wrote this book, because she told me that before learning about the concept of "exceptional self," she didn't have the language to describe it or even think about it. In other words, she didn't always recognize when she was using her strengths, and she had never considered it possible to intentionally choose to activate this version of herself.

Gabriela made me realize that most people don't know that their best self is already within them, they just need to intentionally bring this version to the surface. The positive method was designed to help flip the switch and turn on the qualities that make us truly exceptional.

Once Gabriela recognized her potential through her highlight reel, she became more conscious of when she is, or isn't, bringing her best self into a room. This made her more present in the moment and impactful because she was making an active choice to tap into her strengths each time.

Without a "Who Am I Being?" attitude, it's just so easy to slip into a sleepwalking mode. Especially when what you're good at comes natural to you, it can feel like you don't need to put as much effort into those behaviors. Gabriela had a similar realization, and she identified with how the simple act of checking in with yourself not only engages you in deepening your strengths but makes it more joyful to use them:

> It's easy for me to generally do all those things: Do your job, earn your money, be a good parent. But it makes a huge difference when I'm doing them in a way that is conscious. It makes a difference for me, but also I see it makes a lot of difference for everybody. So it's good enough when I do it kind of okay. I've always been an overachiever, so things get done. But that's the thing: I don't want to just do things well. Now I want to do them joyfully well, you know?

We have many selves, and we have a choice about which one is operating when we enter a room. Learning more about who you are at your best gives you the insight to recognize when you are bringing that version of yourself to the task at hand—whether that is for school, family, work, or pleasure.

Let me give you an example from my own life. I have found there is a lot of variance around how I engage with other people. My highlight reel showed me that when I am exceptional, I have a well of energy that I can tap into that encourages those around me to be themselves, which energizes them. This is sparked by my openness and willingness to reveal what I am feeling, and it often involves humor and helping people look at a situation in a funny way. What I found, however, is that these strengths often take intention to activate. If I am not thinking about it, I can and often do just muddle along and forget to switch these strengths "on." And when they are off, I don't have as much fun, I don't feel as alive, and I am not generating as much energy in other people.

Here are two specific instances where I found I can make a big difference in my life and the lives of others by checking in with myself around who I am being. First, when I go to a meeting at work, it's very easy for me to be passive and let my mind wander. I don't usually like meetings, and often there are ten or more people in our meetings (it could be about a job candidate that we might hire, for example, or it might be a new process for grading exams). Because of how large the meetings are, it can be quite easy for me to tune out and not participate.

But if I make an effort and actively exercise my core strengths, I can improve the meeting by using my openness and expressing my perspective rather than staying quiet and letting myself drift off. I also can use my humor and show people a different way of viewing the issue, improving other people's moods, which improves my own mood. When I do this, I feel much more engaged with the meeting, with other people, and, frankly, with my own life. Only I can decide who I want to be during each meeting, and to experience these benefits I need to make the choice to show up.

A second area where I realized that "switching on" my best self can make a huge difference is entering my own home after work. Because my mind has been focused all day on other things (say, writing, or teaching . . . or meetings!), I often enter my house in a vacant way. If I walk in the door and my kids or my partner Alison is there, I find if I am not intentional I can be very distracted. You know the drill: on the phone checking emails or messages, not asking questions or tuning into the conversation. Unless I am deliberate about activating my strengths, I do not offer my own family the best of myself.

How is it that we can give all our energy and offer up our finest qualities to people we hardly know throughout our day, yet when we are finally home with the people we care for dearly, that part of us suddenly goes into hibernation? This is a form of sleepwalking. When we are present and bring home the characteristics that make us shine, we create deeper connections and meaningful relationships with our family. We share our best with the people we love.

For me, both at work and at home, it takes deliberate intention to activate my strengths and craft my life around them. It involves me putting more energy into each situation. But I find it is more than worth it. My energy levels increase and I affect the people around me in positive ways. And slowly, it becomes a habit of asking myself the question "Who am I being right now?"

★ *Use Every Doorway* ★

To help you think about who you are being as you go through *your* day, every time you walk through a door, touch the physical doorframe as you enter and ask, "Who am I being as I walk in?"

This method allows you to use doorways as natural prompts to check in with who you are projecting into each room or each area of your life. This attitude change is subtle but powerful. It will cause you to adjust your outlook and behaviors in many ways that cannot be scripted or planned. It will help you adapt your unique strengths to each situation at hand and be intentional about who you are being.

Now, write "Doorway Exercise" at the top of a blank page in your practice journal and a date that is sixty-six days from today. During this time period, try to experiment with this attitude as often as possible, with each door you move through. Then, each night before bed, open up your practice journal and spend five minutes writing about how this method is affecting you. Write down which doorways impacted you the most. Which took the most energy for you to summon your best self? What sort of changes did you notice when you intentionally brought your strengths into the room? Did anything surprise you about how others reacted, what was accomplished, or how you felt?

SHAPE YOUR RELATIONSHIPS

Do you remember, from chapter 2, how important our social relationships are when it comes to living a good life and how poor social relationships can be as dangerous to your health as smoking cigarettes? Strong relationships are one of the best predictors of a long, healthy, and fulfilling life. Because of this, it is important that you take a closer look at who you are investing your time, and yourself, with.

It may sound obvious, but many of us end up hanging out with certain people simply because that is who we hang out with. We don't question whether they are bringing out the best, or worst, in us. It's another form of sleepwalking: when habit leads you to continue meeting up with certain people simply because they have been in your life a long time.

Then there are people who help you align your behaviors with the ideal version of yourself. Some people challenge you, energize you, and push you to make a positive impact. You know who these people are because after spending time with them you feel inspired to be authentic. They act as a mirror, reflecting back your potential to you.

Other people put you in a mental state that feels small and cramped. Spending time with them makes you feel bored or listless—or worse: upset and anxious.

Because you absorb the environments and people you surround yourself with, an important part of life crafting is carefully selecting and actively deciding who you want to influence you and your future. As you create the situations and space to exercise your strengths, what relationships do you want to prioritize and who do you want to intentionally have in your life? The following exercise will help you explore this.

★ *Reflect on Your Relationships* ★

Set aside twenty minutes. Open up your calendar or planner—wherever you keep your meetings and events. Go through the last two months. Title a new page in your practice journal "Relationship Shaping," and begin to write down each person with whom you met, called, or video chatted. Then add up the amount of time that you spent with each person over those two months.

What trends do you see emerging? Who do you spend the most time with?

Next, ask yourself, "Who helps make me a better person? Who activates my strengths?" Be honest! It's important to be critical here. This is not saying someone is flawed because they don't activate you and your strengths, but it is acknowledging that some relationships are better for your well-being and build up the person you wish to be, while others don't have that same positive effect.

Now, write down the date sixty-six days out from today in your practice journal. Over the next two months, be intentional about noticing which people help you be your best and which people diminish you.

Take five minutes at the end of each day to keep notes in your practice journal about what you observe. Experiment with scheduling more time with people who activate your best self. Steer clear of people who chip away at your energy and happiness. You also will likely find that new relationships spring out of the new

activities that you added earlier in this chapter. When new relationships seem to activate the best in you, invest time getting to know
those people better.

When you went through the last two months of your calendar,
it is possible that your major takeaway was a realization that you
don't socialize much. That is, you may have learned that you simply do not invest much time in your relationships. But then what
are you spending all your time on? This "social calendar" exercise
helps some people see that they invest all of their time and energy in
their work. It helps others realize they spend more time bingeing on
Netflix than developing relationships.

Only you can decide how you want to spend your time, of
course. But remember: We are transient on this earth. When we
are approaching our end and looking back over life, research says
it is almost certain that good social relationships will be more
meaningful to you than bingeing three seasons of your favorite
TV show alone.

A real benefit of creating your highlight reel is that it reminds
you of the value and meaning of social connections. One of the ways
that you can use this insight is to shift more of your energy into fostering positive relationships. And just as it takes constant watering
to keep a plant healthy, it takes constant meaningful connections to
keep our relationships strong.

Many of us, especially when starting out our careers, or striving to be successful, tend to set aside everything to prioritize work.
Often this means we place our relationships on the back burner.
Emma, a young woman from Charlotte, North Carolina, who had
just made partner in a major consulting firm, recognized that this is
what she had done in her life:

*For so long, life was all deadlines, and needs, and working
on weekends, and working late, and skipping this, skipping*

that. As you're building your career, you kind of emphasize the professional part.

After creating her highlight reel, Emma was struck by how much her family, friends, and colleagues meant to her. So she decided to invest more time in nurturing relationships outside of work. In her words: "When I say reprioritize, I don't mean, 'Okay, work just became a necessary evil' at all. It just means being much more conscious about how to proactively nurture the nonwork relationships and outside-of-work life."

One of my favorite parts of helping people create their highlight reels is bringing them closer to the people they care about. It's valuable to remember how essential our social connections are to our happiness and engagement in life.

GOING BACK TO YOUR HIGHLIGHT REEL

Now that you have your highlight reel, use it as a resource. You can go back to it and use it for self-affirmation in times of self-doubt. It can help you remember how others value you and your strengths anytime you feel the need. This notion of "re-experiencing your highlight reel" may sound almost too easy and obvious. But it's still worth pointing out, because almost half of the people I conducted follow-up interviews with never went back and reread their stories in the years that followed. They treated this experience as a one-off, and that is a real shame.

Think about it more like the way an athlete uses their highlight reel—it's part of your ongoing preparation and practice. Like a pro before a big game, you may find it valuable to revisit your highlight reel before job interviews, presentations, or romantic dates.

Why is it valuable to go back? In addition to a confidence boost and releasing dopamine and good feelings, remember what we covered in chapter 1. Reliving concrete memories of times when you were at your best makes them bright in your mind. The physical linkages and nodes in your brain become stronger and your best self becomes chronically accessible.

USE POSITIVE PSYCHOLOGY TO HELP OTHERS

Now that you have experienced for yourself how powerful the positive method can be, you can use your new insights to light up the people around you. You can help others understand the impact of their strengths.

We have seen how the psychological and social norms behind the eulogy delay can cause us to have a blind spot when it comes to acknowledging people's positive contributions, and even take them for granted. Yet we know how incredibly valuable it is to call out the wonderful things others do and appreciate their gifts. This helps them recognize their potential, create a positive self-image, and improve their relationships.

When we do not actively choose to live a life with gratitude, we can very quickly slip into old patterns and forget to give thanks to the people who enrich our lives. Here is an example from my own life.

My partner Alison and I have been together for a long time. Yet I have found that it is very easy for me to overlook how good she makes me feel when we are together. We have two kids and a busy life. And while I know Alison is the key to what keeps our family life working, when things are going well, it's easy for me to assume away the amazing things that she does as our family's chief operations officer. And if I am not careful, I can forget to acknowledge all that she contributes and just expect it, while only noticing when something is going badly.

Isn't it funny how programmed we are to pinpoint not just our own weaknesses, but to take notice when others do something wrong, and their imperfections? Imagine if you focused on the good someone does for a day. This is bound to improve their lives far more than if we stay fixated on the negative for a whole day. Then you could choose someone else tomorrow and then another person next week to focus on; this is how we slowly create a more gracious and kind world to live in.

One day, as an experiment, I tried to concentrate on how many aspects of our lives would just not work without Alison. At the end of the day, I told her about them and thanked her. A single day of intentionally sharing gratitude does not mean you have created a new habit, of course. But it is how you start one!

The following week, I decided to do this for my friend Bruce, who read an early version of this book. Bruce had taken the time out of his busy schedule to read my manuscript and offer up detailed and honest feedback. While I could have chosen to focus on some of his critical notes, I tried to appreciate the energy and hard work he exerted and his signature strength of expressing himself authentically. I wrote this to him:

> I think one of your strengths is forming strong opinions and letting people know them. I think too many people at our age and professional level only say vanilla things, or simply don't or can't express strong opinions. This makes it a real breath of fresh air talking with you. For example, I love how you let people know that you hate indie music and love Kanye and love pop music. I think I knew these strong opinions within about seven minutes of hanging out with you.

What makes it fun is how you really own your beliefs and you are willing to be open about them. I find it generative and empowering, adding zest to conversation and making life more interesting.

Bruce was surprised that I wrote to him with this mini-living-eulogy. He seemed genuinely touched. I'm sure he could tell it was heartfelt and written specifically for him. This took all of ten minutes to write and send, and it made us both feel closer.

While we may find it intuitive to give thanks to our partners, our family, and our friends, it is also important that we appreciate all the good that our colleagues or peers do. Many of the individuals I interviewed about their highlight reel experience described how they were able to improve their work relationships by noticing and giving gratitude for people's best contributions.

For example, remember Andrew from London, who drove up on Christmas to get his in-laws when they had car trouble? He told me the following:

I've changed the way I reward others, and think of others, and drop people little notes. I remember to tell them when they've done something very well. I spent an hour this morning writing a really nice note to each person on my team, remembering some of the things they've done, thanking them for the support.

It's a small thing, if you think about it, letting people know that you notice and value the unique way they make a difference. But it's actually a very big thing to the people you notice. And as Andrew and many others have told me, it helps their careers by helping them build better relationships. People will come to you and let you know they are genuinely touched that you bothered.

So now that you know more about best selves and the power of gratitude, you have a new approach to improving your life and the lives of people around you. Rather than trying to catch people doing things wrong, you'll find that you create far more positive momentum by catching people doing things right.

★ *Show Your Gratitude* ★

As you go through this week, try to reflect on how often you find yourself "assuming away" people's strengths and contributions. How often do you feel yourself drawn to focus on what others have not done perfectly?

Now, select one person in your life that you appreciate. Pick someone you did not write a gratitude letter to—perhaps one of your children, or a friend, or a work colleague. This week, make it a point to focus on what they do right. On a blank page in your practice journal, take a minute to record some of the good that you notice them doing. What did this person do well in the last few days or weeks that you appreciate, ideally something that shows their signature strengths in action? You can take notes on what you notice about that person as you go through each day, so that you have specific, concrete details.

You are training your brain to look for the positive instead of the limitations and shortcomings.

Then, write to them (or email, or call them—whatever works for you) and tell them. Be specific about what you noticed and why it is so valuable to you. You can make this a quick gratitude letter—think of it as a "lite-highlight"—and send it off.

After you send it and hear back from the person, open up your practice journal and spend ten minutes writing out what you realized from this exercise. What surprised you? What did you notice about your own reactions to writing to the person, and the person's response to your note? Was it hard? How did it make you feel?

In order to make this activity into a habit, try to do this for two months, where you choose one new person to focus on each week. You do not have to always do this extensive of an exercise for each person. Even if you decide to spend a few minutes one day to mentally take note of someone's positive qualities and express this to them, you will find that you are more grateful for them and are deepening your relationship.

YOUR ACHILLES HEEL

This chapter has been all about using your strengths more often. So we need to ask: Is it possible to *overuse* your strengths? Do you think that an overused strength can become an "Achilles heel"?

An Achilles heel usually refers to a weakness in a person that—despite an overall strength—can nevertheless lead to his or her downfall. The phrase emerges from Greek mythology. When Achilles was a baby, fate foretold that he would die young. Guess who didn't like *that* prediction? That's right, his mother.

To prevent his early death, his mom took Achilles to the River Styx, which runs through Hades (which, frankly, is no place to take a child). She took him there because the waters of Styx offer powers of invulnerability. So Achilles's mom held him by his heel and dipped him into the river. Unfortunately, where she held his heel was not touched by the magic waters.

This river dip worked great for Achilles. His power of invulnerability meant that he took many risks in battles and survived, and he became the stuff of legend. But he entered one battle too many, someone shot a poisonous arrow at him, and it hit his heel. And this is how Achilles died early, even despite his magical defensive qualities.

You might be saying, "Clever story, but what's this got to do with me?" Well, maybe *every* strength has a flip side that can become your downfall when it is overused or when not used intelligently.

Take Gabriela from Bogotá, for example. She is an overachiever who has worked hard for the successes in her life. Because of this, Gabriela goes through life with "very high standards" and helps her friends set their sights high as well; this is one of her signature strengths. But what if Gabriela pushes *even harder* into that trait, demanding even higher standards from those around her? Maybe her friends and colleagues begin to think of her as anal-retentive or a perfectionist who is potentially no longer fun to be around because they do not have the freedom to be themselves or relax.

Here's another example of how using a strength to an extreme could become a problem. Remember how Oscar from Stockholm learned from his highlight reel that people really appreciate his assertiveness in speaking the truth? So, let's say Oscar really "turns this up" and uses this strength with his friends and family, but he ends up bulldozing every conversation. As a result, Oscar's network could see him as an overbearing loudmouth who they don't want to spend time with anymore because they can't get a word in.

Since becoming exceptional requires using your strengths more often, you can see why we can't afford to gloss over this topic of the Achilles heel. And in fact, there is some evidence that our strengths could be overdone. For example, a team of researchers led by Huy Le examined the linkage between conscientiousness and job performance. Conscientious people are reliable, dependable, and responsible—all qualities that seem really good for performance on the job.

Well, the data suggested, "yes, to a point." As expected, people with moderate to high conscientiousness performed better in their jobs than people with low conscientiousness. However, the data also suggested that you can have "too much conscientiousness," because people who scored the highest in this trait all performed worse than those who ranged from medium to high. Being hyperconscientious could mean being so focused on the details that not as much gets done.

Similar results emerged in another study about assertiveness. Daniel Ames at Columbia University teamed up with Frank Flynn at Stanford, and showed that leaders who scored high on assertiveness were more likely to lead teams that got more work done. This makes sense: Leaders need to create change and move people toward greater performance. However, assertiveness only works up to a point: The *most* assertive leaders had teams with worse work attitudes and productivity. Too much of a good thing, because employees don't give their best to overbearing bosses they don't like.

I sometimes see "too much of a good thing" happening in my own life. I mentioned before that one of my signature strengths is connecting quickly with people and creating a spark of excitement. I am very extroverted and get a real thrill when I can find a point of connection with someone. This helps me in many ways, like when building friendships and relating with students. I get into conversations with restaurant staff, bartenders, commuters on the train, people waiting in lines in the passport office—anybody. This is a strength that strengthens me—building these connections makes life more enjoyable for me.

If I am not mindful, however, this strength can hurt me. For example, if I am out with my partner Alison on a date, I sometimes spend too much time meeting other people rather than focusing on our conversation. We want to share our ideas with each other and create some new experiences together. So you can imagine how annoying it would be for Alison to sit alone and watch as the person she arrived with entertains strangers.

We can see this phenomenon of overplaying strengths in sports too. Think about what can happen in tennis if your forehand is very strong. You practice your forehand even more, because it feels good to play to your strengths. But you'll lose a lot of matches if you wear out your forehand and are not developing your other skills, like your backhand.

This prompts the question, does focusing on our strengths cause us not to "branch out" and develop new capabilities? And how can you use your strengths without them becoming an Achilles heel?

Your highlight reel builds the confidence you need to experiment with new behaviors and new roles. Using some of the ideas in this chapter, you can push yourself to experiment with a diverse set of activities that let you branch out and stretch your strengths. Not only will this exploration trigger a release of dopamine—a neurotransmitter linked to motivation and pleasure—but it will also give you different insights and perspectives that make you an interesting person. All of this helps you not overuse a single strength or behavior, because you are dividing your time and energy among many areas where you excel. The goal is to have a repertoire of experiences and perspectives where you can use our strengths to contribute something unique and valuable.

The solution to not overusing your strengths is not to turn them down, but to get clear on the impact you are trying to make. You can use your strengths intelligently once you understand the effect you want to have on others and the world around you.

Imagine, for example, a personal coach tells me, "Dan, you are fantastic at connecting with people. On a scale of 1 to 10, you are an 11. But you need to turn yourself down to a 7." By pulling me back, this advice extinguishes my momentum and can make me overly cautious about using this quality. The more I intentionally limit my unique strengths, the less I use behaviors that excite me, and the less I create my unique impact.

It's more effective to say, "Dan, you've got a real strength in connecting with people. Turn that strength up. But instead of pointing it inward ('Meeting people is exciting!'), point it outward ('How can I get others engaged?'). Focus on the outcome that you want to achieve, and use your strengths to move toward that outcome." How this looks in a restaurant when I am focused on interesting conversation with my partner will be different from how this looks when I am speaking to six hundred people at a conference. But the intent of "getting others engaged" is what allows me to channel my strengths in a balanced way.

With his book *Now, Discover Your Strengths*, Marcus Buckingham has helped popularize the focus on developing strengths rather than remediating weaknesses. Buckingham was speaking with Adam Grant, a highly influential writer and speaker, about whether we should ever "turn down" our strengths. This is what Buckingham had to say:

> *You can never have too much of a strength; you can only use it poorly. What we're talking about here is intelligence. You can use your strengths unintelligently. But if you think you can ever have too much of a strength, your coaching then sounds like this: "Be less of yourself."*

Grant relayed a story to me of a time he was giving a student some career advice. At the end of the conversation, after Grant gave her advice, she said, "You're a logic bully." Grant asked her what she meant, and she said, "Well, you just overwhelmed me with rational arguments, and I don't agree with them. But I can't fight back."

At first, Grant thought this was a good thing. He said, "That's my job, right?" The student said, "No, your job is to help me make my own best decision, not to convince me what *your* decision would be." Grant told me this interaction helped him realize that he had failed—at least in his vision of being a mentor.

Some people thought Grant should "turn down" his logic and willingness to share his opinions. But Buckingham told him this:

> *Don't turn that down. Turn that up . . . one of the reasons why people are drawn to you is because you are so purely you—and hopefully over time intelligently you.*

He now helps students see how he would think through the situation, without forcing his answers on them. Using your strengths intelligently is a sustainable way to avoid problems with "overused strengths." Anyone who knows Grant knows that he has not turned down his logic. But by focusing on the outcome he is trying to create, he can apply this strength in different ways. For example, he can use it to simplify tough problems and to help people learn (say, on his podcast *WorkLife*) or use it help students make their own decisions (in his mentor role).

This chapter is full of life-crafting exercises that allow you to practice stretching into your strengths—not to make you feel powerful and gratified, but to help you pursue your potential and create exceptional outcomes. We need to get the most out of our strengths in the spirit of improving our impact in our communities and creating the life we are proud to lead.

CHAPTER 11

Work Crafting

C rafting a life around your strengths requires experimenting with ways to bring them forward across all areas of your life, especially the areas where you spend most of your time. For many people, your job is where you give a big portion of your time and energy. The average person spends more than ninety thousand hours at work in their lifetime—one-third of your entire life! This is why it's important that you feel your work is leveraging your signature strengths, because it allows you to feel more purposeful, positive, and authentic during a huge chunk of your life.

But many people don't feel that way at work. In fact, about 80% of employees across the world say that work is a place where they can't be their best, and they feel like they need to "shut off" in order to get through it.

Does that mean that we should all quit our jobs and start over?

Before we hit the eject button, let's consider some ways we can restructure our work around our strengths a little bit each day, also known as *work crafting*. For many, this is still a pretty new concept. Traditionally, employers created jobs based on what they needed to get accomplished. Nowadays, the way we work has to adapt frequently because the external environment and customers' demands change so fast and so often that organizations have to race to keep up.

As a result, job descriptions are becoming more flexible and personalized. The best way to perform your job responsibilities is now based more on your idiosyncratic strengths and interests and less on what used to work in that job role. The way that one employee or team works may be very different from another employee or team—even when they hold the same job titles.

But it still might not be clear to you, as an individual, how you can craft parts of your job to fit you. Often we think of work as something that we have to do a certain way in order to keep our jobs and pay our bills. The result is that many of us forget that we can adapt the *way* we work without asking permission and without jeopardizing our careers. We can make choices throughout our workday that make use of our strengths, which makes our jobs more meaningful. And when your sense of meaning and enjoyment increases, it usually helps your employer too.

As you may recall from the introduction, when my research team and I had employees in call-center and data-entry roles focus in on their strengths, they felt more authentic and were more satisfied with their jobs. But this also helped the company because they were less likely to quit and they made customers happier.

So the question is, how can you make your work into a stage for using your strengths?

CRAFTING YOUR JOB

When you were hired for your job, you were likely taught a bunch of tasks you need to complete. And no doubt it was important for you to learn how to become proficient in them in order to do your job well. However, that certainly doesn't mean you can only perform those tasks. While it might sound strange to even consider adding more work to your day that hasn't been asked of you, research shows that many employees experience more satisfaction and fulfillment by adding additional roles and tasks that stimulate them, making them more excited to come to work each morning.

To show you what I mean, let me introduce you to Charles, a sales manager at a beer company in the UK. I met Charles when he attended a leadership workshop I taught at London Business School a number of years ago. He had started off as a salesperson at the beginning of his career and was very good at his job. Interacting with people and making a sale always gave him a rush of energy and made him feel alive. Like me, Charles found after completing his highlight reel that building connections was one of his signature strengths.

Charles was so good he soon got a promotion. After only eighteen months he was made sales lead, managing four people. He still was mostly a salesperson, but occasionally his new role meant he had to do some hiring interviews, or get a new hire up to speed, or attend a brewery production meeting. But he said it "didn't get in his way too much," and he continued to enjoy his work. He was promoted again two years later, to sales manager. Now, twenty people reported to him.

The good news for Charles was that he was making about three times more money than when he started. He had a nice new Mercedes and big new office. The bad news was he didn't really like his job anymore. He *hired* people who talked to customers, but he rarely had the chance to talk with customers himself. He spent the majority of his time in what he called "bullshit meetings" and found that he was usually bored at work. He felt like an "order taker"—just processing things that didn't feel meaningful to him.

So, Charles tried an experiment to begin using his strengths at work again. Each week, he decided he would go into the field and visit one client. Not with the intent of selling anything—just to connect with them. One week Charles might go to a supermarket and talk with the manager about what was selling, what was new, what was surprising, or customer trends. Another week he would go to a distributor and talk with people about the trends they were seeing, what was moving in bulk. This was not part of Charles's formal job description. His supervisor didn't ask him to do this. He did this on top of all his regular duties.

Charles enjoyed connecting with clients again, and he was surprised to learn how many other tasks within his job took on more meaning. If he was interviewing a job candidate, he found he now had fresh stories and new examples to talk about. If Charles was meeting with a salesperson about their performance, he could identify more with the market they were facing, and the meeting felt more relevant. If he was sitting in a new product meeting, he could connect the product to the trends he'd talked about with people at the supermarket.

Charles also learned that the best way to make sales is not to try to make sales. Just by using his strengths, and talking with people out of genuine curiosity about the problems they faced, it made people want to do business with him. These "off the normal script" behaviors connected Charles to his customers, and when he was driving back to the office with a new order, he got that emotional charge you get doing something you know you excel in ("Yep. I still got it!").

★ *Create the Job You Want* ★

Think about the activities and conditions in your own job. What tasks activate your signature strengths? What suppresses your best qualities? Now, in your practice journal at the top of a blank page, write "Work Crafting." Underneath, brainstorm some ways you could use your strengths even more at work. Here are some possible ideas and starting points:

Write about all the tasks that already let you use your core strengths, even if it is only a minor part of your role. Can you think up ways to expand these parts of your job, so that you do more of those activities? At first, you might need to invest in these extra activities "on top" of the normal demands. That's okay, because it's likely you'll experience an increase of energy and meaning that will help you in other parts of the job.

Who do you find yourself feeling inspired by at work, and can you find ways to work with them more in the future?

Spend a few weeks incorporating these extra activities into your schedule. Then begin to discuss with your supervisors ways that you can use your strengths more at work. Tell them about ways you've already begun to do this, and why it might be valuable to the organization.

If you can describe new activities that you would like to experiment with, or ways to expand existing parts of your job, your employer might be very interested in working with you on this as part of your "development plan."

Remember, this is not a one-minute makeover. Crafting your strengths into your work does not need to happen all at once. Think about recrafting over the course of a year, or even two years. The important thing is to get started on practicing some new behaviors at work now that use your strengths and help you access your exceptional self more often.

Write the date that is sixty-six days from today in your journal next to your ideas. Now over the next two months, choose one or two of the new behaviors that you brainstormed to practice every day. At the end of each day, take five minutes to make notes in your practice journal about what you observe. What was easy or hard about job crafting for you? What surprised you? What energized you?

CHANGE THE GAME

As the saying goes, "They call it work for a reason." There are always parts of any job that don't seem to connect with our strengths. We often can feel those parts of the job draining us. But it may be possible to use your strengths to *reinterpret* a situation that sucks your energy and make it into a situation that empowers you.

Take Marcus Buckingham, who you may recall helped Adam Grant turn up his strengths in the last chapter. Buckingham is introverted. He dislikes small talk and mingling. As an author and speaker, however, this is part of his role. According to Buckingham, when he mingles at work parties, he worries he is always looking over the other person's shoulder for the other people with whom he should be connecting. He is thinking about how to exit one conversation in order to start the next one. It's exhausting.

But one of Buckingham's signature strengths is curiosity. It turns out he is very good at interviewing because of this. In fact, across his career, he has loved interviewing people and learning what makes them really good at what they do. So, over the years he has learned to reframe "mingling" as "interviewing." At parties now, he selects three people and then conducts three interviews. This approach relieves him of the elements of mingling that used to drain him. He builds real connections with people, and he comes home feeling energized after parties instead of exhausted.

Or take David Holmes, a flight attendant with Southwest Airlines. David started to dread the preflight safety announcements. Sometimes he would have to rattle off the dry, memorized speech six times each day. It got to the point where he delivered the script like he was a robot.

So he re-scripted the announcement using some of his signature strengths: having fun with people and rapping. David began his new act by telling passengers, "We're going to shake things up a bit. I need a little bit of audience participation or this is not going to go over well at all."

At first, many of the customers didn't want to get involved. They wanted to ignore David like they are used to doing. Like we are all used to doing on a flight. In fact, being ignored was part of what made the job so hard for David—it just wore him out. But David got passengers to stomp their feet and clap their hands to make a beat, as he rapped the announcements. He found that by personalizing the announcement as lyrics, and making it fun for the passengers, they listened more and he could bond with them.

He rewrote the normal statement, "In a few moments, the flight attendants will be passing through the cabin to offer you hot or cold drinks. Alcoholic drinks are also available at a nominal charge" to be a rap: "Shortly after takeoff, first things first; there's soft drinks and coffee to quench your thirst. But if you want another kind of drink, then just holler. Alcoholic beverages will be four dollars."

Why did he do this? As David said, "I've had five flights today. I just can't do the normal boring announcement again or I'm going to put myself to sleep."

The airline industry is heavily regulated. There are a number of things that David *needs* to say, by law, or the plane gets grounded and Southwest Airlines gets fined. So he worked hard to find some freedom to use his strengths within the requirements of his job. David said all the things he needed to say as part of the formal requirements—he just said them in his own way.

Because David was using his core skills to explore a new opportunity, he felt enthusiasm and excitement. Emotions are infectious, and passengers picked up on David's energy and responded. Even the passengers who were initially reluctant were smiling, laughing, clapping, and showing David support for bringing his unique strengths to the job.

I've worked with professors who have brought their guitars and singing voices to light up lessons in classes they had become bored with teaching. I have seen traffic officers who brought their dance moves to the streets. These people and those like Charles, Marcus, and David are thriving in areas of their jobs that they used to consider deflating and repetitive, because they found a way to change the game. They found a way to craft even work they disliked into an inspiring opportunity to use their strengths.

PERSONALIZE YOUR JOB TITLE

Your job title is often the first thing you tell people about yourself when you meet them. Job titles can send powerful signals about who we are and what we can do. Your title can also tell others what they might be able to expect from you.

But job titles often feel bureaucratic, and lots of people feel belittled by their titles or that it doesn't reflect their real value. So, I conducted some research with Adam Grant and Justin Berg, professors of organizational behavior, on whether it's possible to develop a job title that is self-affirming. We found that people can craft their own job title that communicates something important about who they are at their best.

For example, Tim is a scheduling counselor at Novant Health, a hospital in North Carolina. He is very good at bringing patients, families, doctors, and staff together. He uses his signature strength of empathy in order to connect the right people together quickly. So, he changed his job title to "The Connector" and started introducing himself that way. Our research showed that Tim and other employees who developed their own job titles around their strengths were less likely to experience burnout on the job—in part because the title helped them project their signature strengths.

Using a strengths-based title not only feels better to Tim, but it also helps the hospital stand out as a special place where their employees care about their work. Some companies are actively encouraging employees to create their own job titles. But even if your employer isn't one of those companies, it's still possible to introduce yourself with an "informal" job name that is based on what you do best.

Consider Theresa, one of the leaders at Novant Health who took part in our job title investigation. Theresa developed and started using the informal title "Office Dance Coordinator" when she introduced herself. This allowed her to highlight her belief that teamwork is like a dance, while reflecting her personal interest in ballroom dance outside the workplace. When meeting new team members, or meeting people outside of work, her informal title generates interest. Theresa said it allows her to express something essential about herself. It is also fine to give yourself a new title and only share it with people you meet outside of work, or with those who are close to you, if that is not the kind of environment you work in. The main objective is to have a title that helps tell a positive story about what you do using your strengths.

★ *Express Yourself in Your Title* ★

Take out your practice journal and spend ten to fifteen minutes brainstorming possible job titles that describe the unique value that *you* bring to the team. Try to come up with possible job titles that incorporate your strengths as well as your personal values, identity, and perspectives. Practice using one of the titles that you brainstormed for a few months. Tell some colleagues or friends about your new title and ask them what they would call themselves. Start using it when you first meet people and they ask what you do. You'll find it leads to positive and interesting discussions about what you really do at work and what you feel you bring to the table.

BRINGING MORE LIFE INTO WORK

When you read your highlight reel, did any of your family and friends write about signature strengths that you do not bring to work? Remember in chapter 8, Ben from Germany found that many of his nonwork contributors mentioned his curiosity as a strength they witnessed, even since his childhood? Unfortunately, he was not bringing that quality into the workplace.

The long-term effects of this were very real for Ben. A few years before completing his highlight reel, Ben started feeling what he called "the Sunday blues." Over the weekend, he started to feel dread as he thought about his upcoming week, and he had trouble getting out of bed Monday mornings. Many of us can identify with Ben's plight. In fact, both my partner Alison and I have felt the same end-of-weekend malaise and sadness at different times in our careers. It is an early warning sign that we have disengaged from what we do.

Once Ben created his highlight reel and recognized that he wasn't bringing his curiosity to his job, he told me he established a new way to think about his workweek. He said, "I now have a little routine on Sunday, thinking about the three things that I'm curious and excited about in the next business week." Ben thinks of conversations with three people that will be inspiring, controversial, and thought-provoking. Then, he actively tries to structure his week around these three conversations.

Ben found that this Sunday exercise energizes him for the week ahead, and now when he thinks of Mondays it lifts him up. He also began to identify areas in his work that didn't spark his curiosity and really bogged his day down:

> *I recognized that I'm not good at doing day-to-day administrative activities. This was really a burden for me. I was always thinking,* Oh, I'm late on submitting my time sheet. I'm always late on doing this project budget. *This was really quite negative for me, like a heavy weight on my shoulder.*

So Ben talked with his supervisor about ways he could bring greater value to the firm by using his strengths more effectively. He negotiated better support in the form of an assistant and focused his energies and time on what he does best: using his curiosity and empathy to have more meaningful conversations with senior executives to solve business problems.

Ben also used the insights from his highlight reel to start bringing curiosity into team meetings. He realized that over the years, he had developed a very strong focus on efficiency and getting right to the point. With his new mindset around curiosity, he encouraged his natural inquisitiveness to come through. In team meetings, Ben now spends time asking and learning something new from his co-workers, even when it isn't essential to finish the project.

Ben not only began feeling more engaged and authentic in his job, but his work improved too. His results and client satisfaction scores became higher than ever, and his team found him to be a more effective leader. When we prioritize our strengths, work starts to feel like an exciting part of life that we get to do, not something we have to do.

★ *Bring Your Strengths to Work* ★

What about you? Can you bring more of your life into your work?

When you analyzed your highlight reel stories in chapter 7, did you find any strengths in your personal life that did not seem to appear in your stories from work colleagues? Take twenty minutes to brainstorm in your practice journal whether there are important parts of you that you are not expressing in your work environment. If there are, what are ways you can restructure the tasks that make up your job to bring those parts of yourself to work more often?

Practice this new behavior for the next few months. At the end of each day, take five minutes to keep notes in your practice journal about what you observed when you tried bringing this strength to your work. Why did you leave this strength "at home" in the past? What assumptions had you made about that strength in a work context, and were any of the assumptions wrong? Did you find using the strength helped at work, or were there negative effects? What surprised you?

YOU AND IKIGAI

This chapter has been all about recrafting your work to align with your strengths. But now, let's turn our focus to an even more important topic. Let's consider your "life's work." How do we know if we are at the right place, the right job? How do we find the thing that we are most passionate about and that is worth committing our time, and sometimes even our lives, to?

One philosophy for finding work that is fulfilling and that drives you to jump out of bed in the morning is a traditional Japanese concept called *ikigai*. Ikigai is a way of living that combines your gifts, what you love to do, and your values to help you give back to the world and experience a meaningful life.

Early in the book, we saw how we live longer when we feel a sense of purpose in what we do. So perhaps we can learn something by looking at communities in the world where people live the longest. Dan Buettner thinks we can. In his book *Blue Zones*, we learn that Japan has some of the longest-living citizens in the world—with most women living to eighty-seven years old and eighty-one years for men. And a remote island called Okinawa, Japan, in the Philippine Sea, has a remarkably high number of centenarians.

Buettner believes that ikigai plays a part in the long lives of people from Okinawa. Although there is no direct English translation of the word, the term "ikigai" embodies "happiness in living." According to Buettner, ikigai is the reason why you get up in the morning. And ikigai is not exclusive to Okinawans: "In all four blue zones such as Sardinia and Nicoya Peninsula, the same concept exists among people living long lives." The French might call it a "raison d'être." Danish people might use the word "hygge."

Think about ikigai as the incredible and deeply satisfying intersection of four qualities:

1. **What I like to do** (without logic or reason, I just like doing these things)
2. **What I'm good at doing** (I have a natural strength in these activities)
3. **What I value** (what is most important to me)
4. **What I can be paid for** (the external world rewards this)

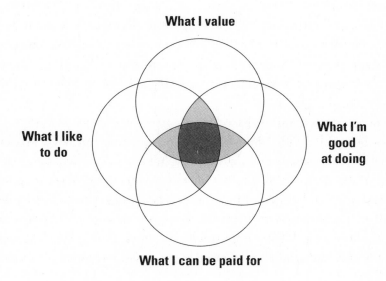

This is how ikigai can help you use your unique talents to give meaning to your days. And when your "life's work" hits all four of these areas, you are giving yourself something enjoyable and motivating to live for. It can energize you, and push you, to share the best of yourself throughout your life. The journey becomes the reward.

After reading this book, the first two elements should be familiar to you. Back in chapter 7, we talked about signature strengths as the overlap between what you *like* to do and what you are *good* at doing. You have spent the last few chapters honing those strengths.

So, now add to this mix the things you *value* the most. What feels crucial to you in life? What is specifically important to you? Usually, you won't know why something seems important—it just is. It doesn't require a reason. In this sense, what we value is more *emotional* than cognitive. For example, I value fun and laughter. I'm sure we could find a logic for how and why laughter is useful, but that is not why I like it. I just value it as part of a good life. So I try to incorporate fun and laughter into my classes and my research meetings.

Finally, what can you be paid to do? In some ways, this is the most obvious consideration, because your life's work also has to allow you to live. Think of this as a balance—there is likely to be a range of activities that you can be paid to do that connect up with the other dimensions. What can you do that lets you earn an income by strengthening yourself? It is an ideal to work toward, of course, but how can you be paid to thrive, doing something that the world needs and that you value?

The intersection of these four elements is your ikigai. Aligning your behaviors with what you like, your talents, and what matters most to you not only gives you clarity, but it also can help you make important choices about how you spend your time. When it comes to work, it can help you think about what projects to pursue, what skills and education to invest in, what jobs to apply for, and what industry to join. Mostly importantly, when you do at last find your ikigai and craft your life around it, you will experience so much more meaning and happiness every day. And according to Dan Buettner, you'll be more likely to live a very long and healthy life.

NOW, GIVE IT ALL AWAY

The purpose of life is to discover your gift.
The work of life is to develop it.
The meaning of life is to give your gift away.

If you have done the hard work throughout this book, then you have discovered and developed your gifts. However, by now you know that the point of the personal highlight reel is not to gloat in your strengths and abilities. And becoming exceptional isn't just about living happier, more fulfilled lives—it's also about brightening the lives of those around us. What you need to do is give your gifts away—that means using your strengths to help the people around you thrive, and improving the piece of the world that is most important to you. Follow your ikigai, and you'll naturally invest your life's energies doing what fulfills you and helps you make your unique impact.

This is what life crafting and work crafting are all about: structuring your activities so you use your unique gifts more often, to increase the positive influence that ripples out from you to others.

But you'd better get started today. Because it's easy to pretend you have forever. It's like when you're on vacation, and it's the beginning of the week. You feel like you have all the time in the world. And then suddenly you're packing your bags to leave. You ask yourself, "Where did the time go?"

When dying patients reach the last weeks of their lives, and they look back on their lives, here are the most frequent things they say:

- "I wish I'd had the courage to live a life true to myself, not the life others expected of me."
- "I wish I'd had the courage to express my feelings."
- "I wish I had stayed in touch with my friends."

Every day is a new opportunity to express yourself, to live authentically, and to connect with the people you love. You have the chance to either shy away from your potential or take a step toward it. So, why wait?

Conclusion

"Death is not the enemy of life, but its friend,
for it is the knowledge that our years are
limited which makes them so precious."

—RABBI JOSHUA L. LIEBMAN

S tanford psychologist Laura Carstensen and her colleagues
conduct studies on how much time people believe they have
left. Some people like to pretend they have forever to live.
Other people are more comfortable recognizing that life is not only
short, but also very fragile. In a research literature of over one hundred studies, the data show that when we accept life's fragility, our
mental focus shifts to the here and now rather than being caught up
in making plans for the future.

Atul Gawande, a cancer surgeon and author of *Being Mortal*,
put it like this:

> *Young people basically aspire to achieve, to get, to have . . .
> When we become aware of the fragility of our life and we
> get older, we focus on a narrower group of friends and fam-
> ily. We become much more focused on intimacy and deeper
> relationships with folks and being connected to a few things
> that make us feel purposeful in the world.*

As we get more comfortable with our transience, we become
motivated to give the best of ourselves to others every day. We are

more likely to strengthen our relationships with the people who mean the most to us.

In fact, this may be why study after study reveal that older people report more positive emotions than younger people, despite lower mobility and declining health. Carstensen coined the term "the positivity effect" for this phenomenon. But get this: The research, which was conducted across different national cultures, shows that it is people's *perspective* about limited time—and not their actual *age*—that shifts their focus and priorities.

It may sound counterintuitive, but—regardless of chronological age—thinking about our limited future enhances our tendency to process information in a positive way. In one experiment, researchers asked participants to complete a writing activity, which directed them to think of time as being either limited or expansive. The participants then looked at some emotional pictures, some of which were positive (a person laughing) and some of which were negative (a car crash). When they later tried to recall the pictures, people could remember more positive pictures when they were thinking of time as limited. And people remembered more negative pictures when they thought of time as infinite. A replication of this experiment showed that the effect was not driven by participants' moods—our brains just seem to scan the environment for the positive when we recognize that our time is limited.

Today, Carstensen is one of the preeminent scholars on longevity, time perspective, and motivation. But when she was twenty-one years old, she was not on a very good life path, as she told me:

> It was the 1970s when I graduated from high school. And what the establishment did was not what I was interested in doing. I was not interested in going to college because that's what people's parents did. I got married right out of high school, and I wasn't even pregnant.

Three years later, Carstensen found herself with a high school education, a young child, and a recent divorce. She told me her top career aspiration at that time was to be an executive assistant, but she feared the more likely path at that point was an alcoholic waitress. Then Carstensen had an experience with life's transience that changed everything.

One night, coming back from seeing the band Hot Tuna in concert in upstate New York, the guy driving the VW minibus she was in crashed, rolling it over an embankment. Carstensen suffered internal bleeding, twenty shattered bones, and major head trauma. She spent four months in the hospital, coming in and out of consciousness for weeks:

I got better enough to realize how close I had come to losing my life, and I saw differently what mattered to me. What mattered to me were other people in my life.

Getting close to her own transience jolted Carstensen onto a better life path. The self-described wild child hunkered down, enrolled at the University of Rochester, got her degree, and eventually earned a PhD in psychology from West Virginia University. Over the next thirty years, Carstensen worked hard, published her research, and became one of the world's leading thinkers on the social psychology of aging.

Over decades of research, the data make it clear: When we get close to life's transience, it motivates us in two ways. First, we work on strengthening the relationships that mean the most to us. Second, we apply the best of ourselves toward something bigger than ourselves. People who connect with life's transience are more likely to take personal responsibility for promoting the welfare of other people, and the next generation, by seeking out work as teachers, mentors, leaders, organizers, and inventors. Awareness of our transience strengthens our desire to invest ourselves in life and work in ways that can outlive the self.

Carstensen thinks the opposite would happen if the length of human life became indefinite. Because if you think you have forever, you take your foot off the gas. As she told me, "It would destroy human motivation if we were immortal. And we'd be miserable. It activates us to think about what we can accomplish before life ends. It helps us get closer to the people around us and makes it more precious to be a living being."

I wrote *Exceptional* because I think the highlight reel process makes it possible to create "positive trauma" that can bring you closer to your transience, all without going through something extreme like a near-death experience. It is deeply meaningful and emotional to hear your own eulogy. These memories from family and friends not only reveal your strengths but can also transform your assumptions about life and relationships, and then help you decide how you want to improve your impact on this world.

Listen: Using your unique strengths gives you the power to improve not just your own life but also the lives of those around you. And you have limited time to use those talents. Sure, if you had infinite time on earth, maybe it would be wise to focus on your weaknesses. After all, with infinite time, maybe we eventually could make all our weaknesses into superpowers.

But guess what? You don't have unlimited time. Going the whole way back to the introduction, I asked you an important question that is central to this book. Now that you have experienced your highlight reel, now that you have walked step by step closer to your potential, I want you to ask yourself this question again: "Given my limited time, what is the best impact I am capable of making in this life?"

Science lends a hand in answering this: Your best contributions won't happen if you dwell on your weaknesses and hamper your confidence. Concentrating on limitations is demotivating. It shuts down our creativity and decision-making abilities.

Instead, when you feel affirmed by your unique strengths and your peak moments, you become energized. You gain the resilience necessary to make positive changes in your life and get the most out of yourself. The positive method is not a "one time" process—after you practice and master a new way to use your signature strengths, it's time to use your growth mindset to find the next way to use your unique strengths to help others even more.

This is how you become exceptional.

Now, it's time to start living a fuller life, an exceptional life, doing exactly what you know you are capable of. Live this way today, again tomorrow, and move toward your potential.

Acknowledgments

Thank you, Alison, for giving me the support and encouragement to study, learn, and write. You're the center of my world! Thank you, Rick Jacobs and Tim Judge, for getting me started as a psychologist, researcher, and professor, and for finding the potential in me. Thank you to everyone at Essentic for creating your positive impact on the world through personal highlight stories, and to Stephanie Loison for helping develop the idea of "paying it forward." I want to thank Eva Avery for her incredible care and creativity throughout the editing process, as well as the Chronicle Prism team, including Mark Tauber, Jennifer Jensen, Pamela Geismar, Cecilia Santini, Beth Weber, and Tera Killip.

Notes

Introduction

1: *As described by neurologist Oliver Sacks:* This Rebecca section is adapted from Sacks, O. 1998. *The Man Who Mistook His Wife for a Hat: And Other Clinical Tales.* New York: Simon & Schuster.

3: *"Remediation":* "When Strength Becomes Weakness," *WorkLife with Adam Grant,* NPR, April 23, 2019, https://one.npr.org/?sharedMediaId =716233761:716233763.

5: *Consider a study I did:* Cable, D. M., Gino, F., Staats, B. 2013. "Breaking Them in or Eliciting Their Best? Reframing Socialization Around Newcomers' Authentic Self-Expression." *Administrative Science Quarterly,* 58: 1–36.

5: *This is why world-class athletes use them:* Weinberg, R. 2008. "Does Imagery Work? Effects on Performance and Mental Skills." *Journal of Imagery Research in Sport and Physical Activity.* DOI: https://doi .org/10.2202/1932-0191.1025.

6: *"I never hit a shot":* Nicklaus, J., McQueen, J. 2005. *Golf My Way.* New York: Simon & Schuster.

6: *This type of imagery:* Gould, D., Guinan, D., Greenleaf, C., Medberry, R., Peterson, K. 1999. "Factors Affecting Olympic Performance: Perceptions of Athletes and Coaches from More and Less Successful Teams." *Sport Psychologist,* 13: 371–394.

Chapter 1. Start with What We Do Right

14: *When people feel defensive and threatened:* Kim, Y. J., Kim, J. 2020. "Does Negative Feedback Benefit (or Harm) Recipient Creativity? The Role of the Direction of Feedback Flow." *Academy of Management Journal,* https://doi .org/10.5465/amj.2016.1196; Seligman, M. 2011. *Flourish.* Boston: Nicholas Brealey, 72–73.

16: *They also experienced substantially less depressive symptoms:* Seligman, M. E. P., Steen, T. A., Park, N., Peterson, C. 2005. "Positive Psychology Progress: Empirical Validation of Interventions." *American Psychologist,* 60: 410–421.

17: *Help people learn about their best impact on others:* Roberts, L. M., Dutton, J. E., Spreitzer, G. M., Heaphy, E. D., Quinn, R. E. 2005. "Composing the Reflected Best-Self Portrait: Building Pathways for Becoming Extraordinary in Work Organizations." *Academy of Management Review,* 30: 712–736.

18: *Research shows that negative events:* Baumeister, R. F., Bratslavsky, E., Finkenauer, C., Vohs, K. D. 2001. "Bad Is Stronger Than Good." *Review of General Psychology,* 5: 323–370.

19: *Using your strengths to make a positive influence:* Waterman, A. S. 1993. "Two Conceptions of Happiness: Contrasts of Personal Expressiveness (Eudaimonia) and Hedonic Enjoyment." *Journal of Personality and Social Psychology,* 64: 678–691.

19: *The people who reflected on unique values:* Dutcher, J. M., Creswell, J. D., Pacilio, L. E., Harris, P. R., Klein, W. M. P., Levine, J. M., Bower, J. E., Muscatell, K. A., Eisenberger, N. I. 2016. "Self-Affirmation Activates the Ventral Striatum: A Possible Reward-Related Mechanism for Self-Affirmation." *Psychological Science,* 27(4): 455–466.

20: *Dopamine is what our body produces:* Cable, D. M. 2018. *Alive at Work.* Brighton, MA: Harvard Business Review Press; Panksepp, J., Wright, J. S., Döbrössy, M. D., Schlaepfer, T. E., Coenen, V. A. 2014. "Affective Neuroscience Strategies for Understanding and Treating Depression: From Preclinical Models to Three Novel Therapeutics." *Clinical Psychological Science,* 2: 472–494.

20: *Positive emotions improve our mental functioning:* Fredrickson, B. 2009. *Positivity.* New York: Random House.

21: *This is why doctors make much more accurate diagnoses:* Achor, S. 2010. *The Happiness Advantage: How a Positive Brain Fuels Success in Work and Life.* New York: Penguin Random House.

21: *Examined these ideas:* Lee, J., Gino, F., Cable, D. M., Staats, B. 2020. "Best-Self Activation and Team Processes." Working paper. *Academy of Management Journal.*

22: *"Emotional labor":* Grandey, A. A. 2003. "When 'the Show Must Go On': Surface Acting and Deep Acting as Determinants of Emotional Exhaustion and Peer-Rated Service Delivery." *Academy of Management Journal,* 46: 86–96.

23: *People feel life has a purpose:* King, L. A., Hicks, J. A., Krull, J. L., Del Gaiso, A. K. 2006. "Positive Affect and the Experience of Meaning of Life." *Journal of Personality and Social Psychology,* 90(1): 179–196; Baumeister, R. F., Landau, M. J. 2018. "Finding the Meaning of Meaning: Emerging Insights on Four Grand Questions." *Review of General Psychology,* 22(1): 1–10; Heintzelman, S. J., Trent, J., King, L. A. 2013. "Encounters with Objective Coherence and the Experience of Meaning in Life." *Psychological Science,* 24(6): 991–998.

24: *It's very difficult to be an inspiring role model:* Cheung, C. S. S., Pomerant, E. M. 2012. "Why Does Parents' Involvement Enhance Children's Achievement? The Role of Parent-Oriented Motivation." *Journal of Educational Psychology,* 104: 820–832; McPherson, G. E. 2008. "The Role of Parents in Children's Musical Development." *Psychology of Music,* 37: 91–110.

24: *It's hard to inspire others:* Conger, J. A. 1991. "Inspiring Others: The Language of Leadership." *Academy of Management Executive,* 5: 31–45.

Chapter 2. The Hidden Forces That Limit Us

26: *Digital eulogy:* "The Month I Died: Reading My Own Eulogies," *Medium,* December 20, 2016, https://medium.com/dose/the-month-i-died-reading-my-own-eulogies-f8d83b8d07f2.

29: *The stories we use to describe ourselves:* Ruvolo, A., Markus, H. 1992. "Possible Selves and Performance: The Power of Self-Relevant Imagery." *Social Cognition,* 10: 95–124.

29: *The best way to improve our social relationships:* Kumar, A., Epley, N. 2018. "Undervaluing Gratitude: Expressers Misunderstand the Consequences of Showing Appreciation." *Psychological Science,* 29: 1423–1435.

29: *When it comes to enjoying life:* Diener, E., Seligman, M. E. P. 2002. "Very Happy People." *Psychological Science,* 13: 81–84.

29: *Not having good relationships:* Holt-Lunstad, J., Smith, T. B., Layton, J. B. 2010. "Social Relationships and Mortality Risk: A Meta-Analytic Review." *PLOS Medicine,* 7(7), Article e1000316. doi:10.1371/journal.pmed.1000316.

30: *Most people try to keep this truth:* Solomon, S., Greenberg, J., Pyszczynski, T. 2015. *The Worm at the Core.* New York: Penguin; Becker, E. 1973. *The Denial of Death.* New York: Free Press.

30: *Our subconscious knows when we are idling:* Wilson, T. D. 2002. *Strangers to Ourselves: Discovering the Adaptive Unconscious.* Cambridge, MA: Belknap Press of Harvard University Press.

30: *"Existential regret":* Lucas, M. 2004. "Existential Regret: A Crossroads of Existential Anxiety and Existential Guilt." *Journal of Humanistic Psychology,* 44: 58–70.

30: *Dave began to live a better version of his self:* "The Month I Died: Reading My Own Eulogies," *Medium,* December 20, 2016, https://medium.com/dose /the-month-i-died-reading-my-own-eulogies-f8d83b8d07f2.

30: *He invented dynamite:* Andrews, E. "Did a Premature Obituary Inspire the Nobel Prize?" *History,* December 9, 2016, https://www.history.com/news /did-a-premature-obituary-inspire-the-nobel-prize.

31: *A "merchant of war":* Fant, K. 2006. *Alfred Nobel: A Biography.* New York: Arcade Publishing.

31: *Working for his resume:* Brooks, D. "Should You Live for Your Resume— Or Your Eulogy?" TedTalk, March 2014, https://www.ted.com/talks/david _brooks_should_you_live_for_your_resume_or_your_eulogy?language=en.

38: *It's why most adults still haven't arranged a will:* Walls, B. L. "Haven't Done a Will Yet?" AARP, February, 24, 2017, https://www.aarp.org/money /investing/info-2017/half-of-adults-do-not-have-wills.html.

Chapter 3. Possible Selves

41: *Over the last fifty thousand years:* Harari, Y. N. 2014. *Sapiens: A Brief History of Humankind.* London: Random House.

42: *Aileen described her relationship:* Streep, P. "The Enduring Pain of Childhood Verbal Abuse," *Psychology Today,* November 14, 2016, https:// www.psychologytoday.com/us/blog/tech-support/201611/the-enduring-pain -childhood-verbal-abuse.

43: *Different elements of our self:* Markus, H., Wurf, E. 1987. "The Dynamic Self-Concept: A Social Psychological Perspective." *Annual Review of Psychology,* 38(1): 299–337.

44: *"Who am I?":* Thoits, P. A. 1991. "On Merging Identity Theories and Stress Research." *Social Psychology Quarterly,* 54: 101–112.

44: *Our dreaded possible selves:* Markus, H., Nurius, P. 1986. "Possible Selves." *American Psychologist*, 41: 954–969.

45: *How we can edit our personal stories:* Oyserman, D., Bybee, D., Terry, K. 2006. "Possible Selves and Academic Outcomes: How and When Possible Selves Impel Action." *Journal of Personality and Social Psychology*, 91(1): 188–204.

45: *Society floods us with stories:* Thomas, D., Townsend, T., Belgrave, F. 2003. "The Influence of Cultural and Racial Identification on the Psychosocial Adjustment of Inner-City African American Children in School." *American Journal of Community Psychology*, 32: 217–228.

45: *High school students:* Kao, G. 2000. "Group Images and Possible Selves among Adolescents: Linking Stereotypes to Expectations by Race and Ethnicity." *Sociological Forum*, 15: 407–430.

48: *Associative models of memory:* Anderson, J. R. 1983. *The Architecture of Cognition.* Cambridge, MA: Harvard University Press; Wyer, R. S., Srull, T. K. 1989. "Person Memory and Judgment." *Psychological Review*, 96: 58–83.

49: *The brain can change:* Storr, W. "You Can Think Your Way into Changing— But There Are Limits," *Quartz*, December 15, 2015, https://qz.com/581044 /you-can-think-your-way-into-changing-who-you-are-but-there-are-limits.

50: *Alcoholics are less likely to relapse:* Brownell, K. D., Marlatt, G. A., Lichtenstein, E., Wilson, G. T. 1986. "Understanding and Preventing Relapse." *American Psychologist*, 41: 765–782.

51: *Develop a different narrative:* Stephens, N. M., Hamedani, M. Y. G., Destin, M. 2014. "Closing the Social-Class Achievement Gap: A Difference-Education Intervention Improves First-Generation Students' Academic Performance and All Students' College Transition." *Psychological Science*, 25: 943–953.

52: *If you replace negative stories:* Selk, J. 2008. *10-Minute Toughness.* New York: McGraw-Hill Education. Selk is an influential coach who helps athletes create personal highlight reels. Selk became a go-to coach for professional and Olympic athletes seeking mental coaching. He also was director of mental training for the St. Louis Cardinals, when they won two World Championships in a six-year period.

55: *When your best self is activated:* Lord, R. G., Hall, R. J. 2005. "Identity, Deep Structure, and the Development of Leadership Skill." *Leadership Quarterly*, 16(4): 591–615; Oyserman D., Smith, E. K. G. 2012. "Self, Self-Concept, and Identity." In M. R. Leary and J. P. Tangney (Eds.), *Handbook of Self and Identity* (pp. 69–104). New York: Guilford Press.

Chapter 4. Changing Your Story Once It's in Motion

57: *The reality and power of habit:* Ghoshal was professor of strategy at the London Business School. You can watch his talk here: "The Smell of the Place," YouTube, March 3, 2010, https://www.youtube.com/watch?v =UUddgE8rI0E.

58: *"When is somebody going to build this library?":* "The Room of Requirement," *This American Life*, December 28, 2018, https://www.thisamericanlife .org/664/the-room-of-requirement.

60: *Post-traumatic growth:* Tedeschi, R., Calhoun, L. 2004. "Posttraumatic Growth: Conceptual Foundations and Empirical Evidence." *Psychological Inquiry*, 15: 1–18; "Crucibles of Leadership," *Harvard Business Review*, September 2002, https://hbr.org/2002/09/crucibles-of-leadership.

60: *Between 58% and 83% of participants report growth after trauma:* Jayawickreme, E., Blackie, L. E. R. 2016. *Exploring the Psychological Benefits of Hardship: A Critical Reassessment of Posttraumatic Growth.* Cham, Switzerland: Springer.

60: *As a result of his son's death:* Mangelsdorf, J., Eid, M., Luhmann, M. 2018. "Does Growth Require Suffering? A Systematic Review and Meta-Analysis on Genuine Posttraumatic and Postecstatic Growth." *Psychological Bulletin*, 145(3): 302–338.

63: *"The challenge of mindfulness":* Foley, B. "What You Own, Owns You: Minimalism for People Who Love Things," *Medium*, June 8, 2017, https:// medium.com/personal-growth/what-you-own-owns-you-minimalism-for-peo-ple-who-love-things-5a083a7e14f3.

64: *We can gain wisdom:* Park, C. L., Cohen, L. H., Murch, R. L. 1996. "Assessment and Prediction of Stress-Related Growth." *Journal of Personality*, 64: 71–105; Janoff-Bulman, R. 1992. *Shattered Assumptions: Towards a New Psychology of Trauma*. New York: Free Press.

66: *Only about 25% of post-traumatic growth studies:* Mangelsdorf, J., Eid, M., Luhmann, M. 2018. "Does Growth Require Suffering? A Systematic Review and Meta-Analysis on Genuine Posttraumatic and Postecstatic Growth." *Psychological Bulletin*, 145(3): 302–338.

67: *The growth reveals itself:* Roepke, A. M. 2013. "Gains without Pains? Growth after Positive Events." *Journal of Positive Psychology*, 8: 280–291; Taubman-Ben-Ari, O., Findler, L., Sharon, N. 2011. "Personal Growth in Mothers: Examination of the Suitability of the Posttraumatic Growth Inventory as a Measurement Tool." *Women & Health*, 51: 604–622.

67: *Although some researchers argue that negative life events:* Baumeister, R. F., Bratslavsky, E., Finkenauer, C., Vohs, K. D. 2001. "Bad Is Stronger Than Good." *Review of General Psychology*, 5: 323–370.

67: *Your personal highlight reel can trigger post-traumatic:* Roberts, L. M., Dutton, J. E., Spreitzer, G. M., Heaphy, E. D., Quinn, R. E.. 2005. "Composing the Reflected Best-Self Portrait: Building Pathways for Becoming Extraordinary in Work Organizations." *Academy of Management Review*, 30: 712–736.

67: *Research suggests that you might feel:* Sheldon, K. M., Lyubomirsky, S. 2006 "How to Increase and Sustain Positive Emotion: The Effects of Expressing Gratitude and Visualizing Best Possible Selves." *Journal of Positive Psychology*, 1: 73–82.

68: *"In the face of adversity":* Spreitzer, G. M. 2006. "Leading to Grow and Growing to Lead: Leadership Development Lessons from Positive Organizational Studies." *Organizational Dynamics*, 35: 305–315.

Chapter 5. Put Your Best Dress in the Window

75: *It does this by helping us overcome:* Steele, C. M. 1988. "The Psychology of Self-Affirmation: Sustaining the Integrity of the Self." *Advances in Experimental Social Psychology*, 21: 261–302; Cohen, G. L., Sherman., D. K. 2014. "The Psychology of Change: Self-Affirmation and Social Psychological Intervention." *Annual Review of Psychology*, 65: 333–371.

76: *Pride in the Oxford dictionary:* "Pride," Lexico, https://en.oxforddictionaries.com/definition/pride.

77: *Parents are expected to punish conceit:* Arcia, E., Reyes-Blanes, M. E., Vazquez-Montilla, E. 2000. "Constructions and Reconstructions: Latino Parents' Values for Children." *Journal of Child and Family Studies*, 9(3): 333–350.

77: *Groups and teams punish arrogance:* Anderson, C., Srivastava, S., Beer, J. S., Spataro, S. E., Chatman, J. A. 2006. "Knowing Your Place: Self-Perceptions of Status in Face-to-Face Groups." *Journal of Personality and Social Psychology*, 81: 1094–1110.

81: *She defines pride:* Fredrickson, B. L. 2013. "Positive Emotions Broaden and Build." In P. Devine and A. Plant (Eds.), *Advances in Experimental Social Psychology* (vol. 47, pp. 1–53). Burlington, VT: Academic Press.

82: *"If you are trying to pretend":* Dyson, M. E. "The Seven Deadly Sins: Pride," NPR, February 13, 2006, https://www.npr.org/templates/story/story.php?storyId=5203925.

82: *When it feels difficult to bring stories to mind:* Oyserman, D., Bybee, D., Terry, K. 2006. "Possible Selves and Academic Outcomes: How and When Possible Selves Impel Action." *Journal of Personality and Social Psychology,* 91(1): 188–204.

83: *Writing about our experiences:* King, L. A. 2002. "Gain without Pain? Expressive Writing and Self-Regulation." In S. J. Lepore and J. M. Smyth (Eds.), *The Writing Cure: How Expressive Writing Promotes Health and Emotional Well-Being* (119–134). Washington, DC: American Psychological Association.

84: *You need to remember:* Rose, T., Ogas, O., "How Can You Uncover Your Best Self? Start by Judging Other People—Really," Ideas.Ted.com, October 30, 2018, https://ideas.ted.com/how-can-you-uncover-your-best-self -start-by-judging-other-people-really.

84: *Just thinking about these events:* Redirect, W. T., Pennebaker, J. W. 2004. *Writing to Heal: A Guided Journal for Recovering from Trauma and Emotional Upheaval.* Oakland, CA: New Harbinger Press.

84: *Research on this type of expressive writing:* Burton C. M., King, L. A 2004. "The Health Benefits of Writing about Intensely Positive Experiences." *Journal of Research in Personality,* 38(2): 150–163; King, L. 2001. "The Health Benefits of Writing about Life Goals." *Personality and Social Psychology Bulletin,* 27: 798–807; Pennebaker, J. W., Seagal, J. D. 1999. "Forming a Story: The Health Benefits of Narrative." *Journal of Clinical Psychology,* 55(10): 1243–1254.

85: *Our brains are literally built for stories:* Harari, Y. N. 2014. *Sapiens: A Brief History of Humankind.* London: Random House; Boris, V. "What Makes Storytelling So Effective for Learning," *Harvard Business Publishing,* December 20, 2017, https://www.harvardbusiness.org/what-makes-storytelling-so -effective-for-learning.

85: *Research by Joanne Wood:* Wood, J. V., Perunovic, W. Q. E., Lee, J. W. 2009. "Positive Self-Statements: Power for Some, Peril for Others." *Psychological Science,* 20: 860–866.

86: *This new identity:* Cohen, G. L., Sherman., D. K. 2014. "The Psychology of Change: Self-Affirmation and Social Psychological Intervention." *Annual Review of Psychology,* 65: 333–371.

Chapter 6. Create Your Personal Highlight Reel

89: *Gratitude creates norms of reciprocity:* McCullough, M. E., Emmons, R. A., Tsang, J. 2002. "The Grateful Disposition: A Conceptual and Empirical Typology." *Journal of Personality and Social Psychology,* 82: 112–127.

89: *Books that have been digitized by Google:* Kesebir, P., Kesebir, S. 2012. "The Cultural Salience of Moral Character and Virtue Declined in 20th Century America." *Journal of Positive Psychology*, 7: 471–480.

89: *When we focus on what we are grateful for:* Emmons, R. A., McCullough, M. E. 2003. "Counting Blessings versus Burdens: An Experimental Investigation of Gratitude and Subjective Well-Being in Daily Life." *Journal of Personality and Social Psychology*, 84: 377–389; Seligman, M. E. P., Steen, T. A., Park, N., Peterson, C. 2005. "Positive Psychology Progress: Empirical Validation of Interventions." *American Psychologist*, 60: 410–421; Mongrain, M., Anselmo-Matthews, T. 2012. "Do Positive Psychology Exercises Work? A Replication of Seligman et al. (2005)." *Journal of Clinical Psychology*, 68(4): 382–389.

104: *"From my earliest memories":* Miller, B. J. "How to Give a Eulogy That Truly Celebrates the Person You Are Honoring," Ideas.Ted.com, July 23, 2019, https://ideas.ted.com/how-to-give-a-eulogy-that-truly-celebrates-the-person-youre-honoring.

Chapter 7. Discover Your Best Impact

116: *The act of drawing or representing the memory:* Wammes, J. D., Meade, M. E., Fernandes, M. A. 2016. "The Drawing Effect: Evidence for Reliable and Robust Memory Benefits in Free Recall." *Quarterly Journal of Experimental Psychology*, 69: 1752–1776.

116: *An additional form of processing:* Herrera, T. "A Simple Way to Remember Things: Draw a Picture," *New York Times*, January 6, 2019, https://www.nytimes.com/2019/01/06/smarter-living/memory-tricks-mnemonics.html.

117: *They are more about your core capacities:* Battey, S. "The VIA Survey: 7 Ways to Recognize Your Strengths and Act on Them," *Positive Psychology*, April 7, 2019, https://positivepsychology.com/via-survey.

117: *"A strength is more than a skill":* "When Strength Becomes Weakness," *WorkLife with Adam Grant*.

120: *"Hallmarks" of strengths:* Seligman, M. 2011. *Flourish*. Boston: Nicholas Brealey, 72–73; also see Battey, S., "The VIA Survey: 7 Ways to Recognize Your Strengths and Act on Them," *Positive Psychology*, April 7, 2019, https://positivepsychology.com/via-survey.

123: *Universal Strengths determined by Martin Seligman and his colleagues:* Seligman, M. E .P., Steen, T. A., Park, N., Peterson, C. 2005. "Positive Psychology Progress: Empirical Validation of Interventions." *American Psychologist*, 60: 410–421.

Chapter 8. Hear Your Own Eulogy

140: *I think deep down:* "When Strength Becomes Weakness," *WorkLife with Adam Grant.*

141: *"Self-verification":* Swann, W. B. 1983. "Self-Verification: Bringing Social Reality into Harmony with the Self." In J. Suls and A. G. Greenwald (Eds.), *Psychological Perspectives on the Self* (vol. 2, pp. 33–66). Hillsdale, NJ: Erlbaum; Cable, D. M., Kay, V. 2012. "Striving for Self-Verification during Organizational Entry." *Academy of Management Journal,* 55: 360–380.

145: *Back in 1978, psychologists described imposter syndrome:* Clance, P. R., & Imes, S. A. 1978. "The imposter phenomenon in high achieving women: Dynamics and therapeutic intervention." *Psychotherapy: Theory, Research & Practice,* 15(3), 241–247.

146: *Turns out that many people suffer:* Johnson, W. B., Smith, D. G. "Mentoring Someone with Imposter Syndrome," *Harvard Business Review,* February 22, 2019, https://hbr.org/2019/02/mentoring-someone-with-imposter-syndrome.

146: *"No matter who we are":* "Tom Hanks Says Self-Doubt Is a 'Hire-Wire Act That We All Walk,'" NPR, April 26, 2016, https://www.npr .org/2016/04/26/475573489/tom-hanks-says-self-doubt-is-a-high-wire-act-that -we-all-walk?t=1550934665484.

147: *The imposter syndrome:* Richards, C. "Learning to Deal with the Imposter Syndrome," *New York Times,* October 26, 2015, https://www.nytimes .com/2015/10/26/your-money/learning-to-deal-with-the-impostor-syndrome .html.

147: *According to my colleague Herminia Ibarra:* Ibarra, H. 2015. *Act Like a Leader, Think Like a Leader.* Brighton, MA: Harvard Business Review Press.

148: *The problem with this mindset:* Dweck, D. S. 2006. *Mindset: How We Can Learn to Fulfill our Potential.* New York: Ballantine Books.

148: *Women and minorities often may be hit the hardest:* Johnson, W. B., Smith, D. G. "Mentoring Someone with Imposter Syndrome."

154: *Whenever people visited Seligman's website:* Seligman, M. E .P., Steen, T. A., Park, N., Peterson, C. 2005. "Positive Psychology Progress: Empirical Validation of Interventions." *American Psychologist,* 60: 410–421.

154: *He told one group to take that online survey:* You can take the inventory here: "The VIA Character Strengths Survey," http://www.viacharacter.org /www/Character-Strengths-Survey.

155: *Replicated Seligman's findings:* Mongrain, M., Anselmo-Matthews, T. "Do Positive Psychology Exercises Work?"

Chapter 9. Stretching into Our Strengths

161: *To do this, they must learn:* Maguire, E. A., Woollett, K., Spiers, H. J. 2006. "London Taxi Drivers and Bus Drivers: A Structural MRI and Neuropsychological Analysis." *Hippocampus*, 16: 1091–1101.

162: *The magic here is that we can cause our neurons:* Gravitz, L. "The Forgotten Part of Memory," *Nature*, July 24, 2019, https://www.nature.com/articles/d41586-019-02211-5; https://qz.com/581044/you-can-think-your-way-into-changing-who-you-are-but-there-are-limits.

162: *Information zooms quickly:* Sapolsky, R. M. 2017. *Behave: The Biology of Humans at Our Best and Worst.* New York: Penguin Press.

162: *This is called automaticity:* Bargh, J. A. 1997. *The Automaticity of Everyday Life.* Mahwah, NJ: Lawrence Erlbaum Associates.

164: *Stretching into your strengths:* Ibarra, H. *Act Like a Leader, Think Like a Leader.*

165: *I subscribe to "humble leadership":* Cable, D. M. "How Humble Leadership Really Works." *Harvard Business Review*, April 23, 2018, https://hbr.org/2018/04/how-humble-leadership-really-works.

167: *The way you interpret it makes all the difference:* Dweck. *Mindset: How We Can Learn to Fulfill Our Potential.*

168: *Authenticity trap:* Ibarra, H. *Act Like a Leader, Think Like a Leader.*

169: *We gain resilience in the face of temporary challenges:* Markus, H., Nurius, P. 1986. "Possible Selves." *American Psychologist*, 41: 963.

169: *Visualize themselves being successful:* Ruvolo, A., Markus, H. 1992. "Possible Selves and Performance: The Power of Self-Relevant Imagery." *Social Cognition*, 10: 95–124.

170: *Write about one of four topics for twenty minutes each day:* King, L. 2001. "The Health Benefits of Writing about Life Goals." *Personality and Social Psychology Bulletin*, 27: 798–807.

173: *They observed undergraduates:* Pham, L. B., Taylor, S. E. 1999. "From Thought to Action: Effects of Process- versus Outcome-Based Mental Simulations on Performance." *Personality and Social Psychology Bulletin*, 25: 250–260; another good example showing how envisioning success leads to success is Sherman, S. J., Skov, R. B., Hervitz, E. F., Stock, C. B. 1981. "The Effects of Explaining Hypothetical Future Events: From Possibility to Actuality and Beyond." *Journal of Experimental Social Psychology*, 17: 142–158.

174: *People's positive fantasies diminished success in a weight loss program:* Oettingen, G., Wadden, T. A. 1991. "Expectation, Fantasy, and Weight Loss: Is the Impact of Positive Thinking Always Positive?" *Cognitive Therapy and Research*, 15: 167–175.

174: *By fantasizing about the outcome:* Oettingen, G., Wadden, T. A. 1991. "Expectation, Fantasy, and Weight Loss."

175: *People who were interested in forming a healthy new habit:* Phillippa, L., van Jaarsveld, C. H. M., Potts, H. W. W., Wardle, J. 2010. "How Are Habits Formed: Modelling Habit Formation in the Real World." *European Journal of Social Psychology*, 40: 998–100.

Chapter 10. Life Crafting

182: *Here are just a few examples, inspired by Martin Seligman's:* Seligman, M. 2011. *Flourish: A Visionary New Understanding of Happiness and Well-Being.* New York: Atria.

197: *Examined the linkage between conscientiousness and job performance:* Le, H., OH, I.-S., Robbins, S. B., Ilies, R., Holland, E., Westrick, P. 2010. "Too Much of a Good Thing? The Curvilinear Relationships between Personality Traits and Job Performance." *Journal of Applied Psychology*, 95: 1–21.

198: *Assertiveness only works up to a point:* Ames, D. R., Flynn, F. J. 2007. "What Breaks a Leader? The Curvilinear Relation between Assertiveness and Leadership." *Journal of Personality and Social Psychology*, 92: 307–324.

200: *You can never have too much of a strength:* "When Strength Becomes Weakness," *WorkLife with Adam Grant.*

Chapter 11. Work Crafting

203: *The average person spends more than ninety thousand hours:* "One Third of Your Life Is Spent at Work," *Gettysburg*, https://www.gettysburg.edu/news/stories?id=79db7b34-630c-4f49-ad32-4ab9ea48e72b&pageTitle=1%2F3+of+your+life+is+spent+at+work.

203: *About 80% of employees:* Cable, D. M. 2018. *Alive at Work: The Neuroscience of Helping Your People Love What They Do.* Boston, MA: Harvard Business School Press.

203: *Work crafting:* Wrzesniewski, A., Dutton, J. E. 2001. "Crafting a Job: Revisioning Employees as Active Crafters of Their Work." *Academy of Management Review*, 26: 179–201; Tims, M., Derks, D., Bakker, A. B. 2016.

"Job Crafting and Its Relationships with Person–Job Fit and Meaningfulness: A Three-Wave Study." *Journal of Vocational Behavior,* 92: 44–53.

204: *When your sense of meaning and enjoyment increases:* Cable, D. M. 2018. *Alive at Work.*

204: *This also helped the company:* Cable, D. M., Gino, F., Staats, B. 2013. "Reinventing Employee Onboarding." *MIT Sloan Management Review,* 54: 23–28. Reprint 54321.

204: *While it might sound strange:* Wrzesniewski, A., LoBuglio, N., Dutton, J. E., Berg, J. M. 2013. "Job Crafting and Cultivating Positive Meaning and Identity in Work. In A. B. Bakker (Ed.), *Advances in Positive Organizational Psychology* (pp. 281–302). Bingley, UK: Emerald Group Publishing.

206: *Here are some possible ideas:* If you want to dive even deeper into this process, visit: "The Business of +," Center for Positive Organizations, http://www.bus.umich.edu/Positive/POS-Teaching-and-Learning/JobCraftingExercise.htm.

208: *He dislikes small talk:* "When Strength Becomes Weakness," *WorkLife with Adam Grant.*

208: *So he re-scripted the announcement:* "Rapping Flight Attendant," YouTube, June 13, 2009, http://www.youtube.com/watch?v=U_yW1zdQzaY.

209: *Traffic officers who brought their dance moves:* "Dancing Policeman, Philippines," YouTube, October 31, 2008, http://www.youtube.com/watch?v=344U4zbYqHU.

210: *People can craft their own job title:* Grant, A., Berg, J., Cable, D. M. 2014. "Job Titles as Identity Badges: How Self-Reflective Titles Can Reduce Emotional Exhaustion." *Academy of Management Journal,* 57: 1201–1225.

211: *Some companies are actively encouraging employees:* "Creative Job Titles Can Energize Workers," *Harvard Business Review,* May 2006, https://hbr.org/2016/05/creative-job-titles-can-energize-workers.

215: *Ikigai is the reason why you get up:* Mitsuhashi, Y. "Ikigai: A Japanese Concept to Improve Work and Life," *BBC Worklife,* August 7, 2017, https://www.bbc.com/worklife/article/20170807-ikigai-a-japanese-concept-to-improve-work-and-life.

217: *The meaning of life:* Viscott, D. 1993. *Finding Your Strength in Difficult Times: A Book of Meditations.* Chicago: Contemporary Books.

217: *When dying patients reach the last weeks:* Ware, B. 2011. *The Top Five Regrets of the Dying.* Sydney, Australia: Hay House.

Conclusion

219: *We become much more focused on intimacy:* Klein, E. "9 Lessons a Physician Learned about Dying," *Vox,* March 26, 2015, https://www.vox.com/2014/10/21/7023257/atul-gawande-taught-me-dying-being-mortal.

220: *We are more likely to strengthen our relationships:* Carstensen, L. L. 2006. "The Influence of a Sense of Time on Human Development." *Science,* 312: 1913–1915.

220: *Older people report more positive emotions:* Carstensen, L. L., Turan, B., Scheibe, S., Ram, N., Ersner-Hershfield, H., Samanez-Larkin, G. R., Nesselroade, J. R. 2011. "Emotional Experience Improves with Age: Evidence Based on over 10 Years of Experience Sampling." *Psychology and Aging,* 26(1): 21–33.

220: *The effect was not driven by participants' moods:* Barber, S. J., Opitz, P. C., Martins, B., Sakaki, M., Mather, M. 2016. "Thinking about a Limited Future Enhances the Positivity of Younger and Older Adults' Recall: Support for Socioemotional Selectivity Theory." *Memory and Cognition,* 44: 869–882.

221: *I got better enough to realize:* Pomerantz, D., "Rethinking Old Age," *Forbes,* November 10, 2007, https://www.forbes.com/forbes/2007/1126/122.html#10710f0c5d88.

221: *People who connect with life's transience:* Grant, A. M., Wade-Benzoni, K. M. 2009. "The Hot and Cool of Death Awareness at Work: Mortality Cues, Aging, and Self-Protective and Prosocial Motivations." *Academy of Management Review,* 34(4): 600–622; McAdams, D. P., de St. Aubin, E. 1992. "A Theory of Generativity and Its Assessment through Self-Report, Behavioral Acts, and Narrative Themes in Autobiography." *Journal of Personality and Social Psychology,* 62: 1003–1015.